Canvas— 3141

Narmi
252

# Stories With a Twist

## Second Edition

## by Natalie Hess

D1227420

ALTA BOOK CENTER PUBLISHERS

| | |
|---|---|
| *Acquisitions Editor:* | Aaron Berman |
| *Content Editor:* | Jean Zukowski Faust |
| *Production Editor:* | Jamie Ann Cross |
| *Cover and Interior Art:* | Kathleen Peterson |
| *Interior Design:* | Cleve Gallat |

© 1999 Alta Book Center Publishers, First Edition
© 2006 Alta Book Center Publishers, Second Edition

All rights reserved. No part of this book may be reproduced or
transmitted in any form or by any means without permission in
writing from the publisher. This restriction includes, but is not
limited to, reproduction for educational or classroom purposes.

Alta Book Center Publishers
14 Adrian Court
Bulingame, California 94010 USA
Phone: 800 ALTA/ESL • 650.692.1285—*Int'l*
Fax: 800 ALTA/FAX • 650.692.4654—*Int'l*
Email: info@altaesl.com • Website: www.altaesl.com

ISBN 978-1-882483-96-9

# ✽ Contents

*To*

*My colleagues at Northern Arizona University in Yuma*

*and Arizona Western College.*

*Let's make happy stories together.*

# ❋ To the Teacher

## *Introduction*

I WROTE THIS BOOK because I needed it. I needed an interesting and viable book for my high beginning and lower intermediate students. I wanted a book that would interest them; activate them; not talk down to them; and make them read, write, listen, think, and reflect on their own lives—their hopes, their fears, their ambitions, and their doubts—all while they were learning the complicated and demanding English language.

No book, of course, can really fulfill all the goals that I've so blithely spelled out in the preceding paragraph. For a book—or any text—to do all that, it needs a creative, motivated, and dedicated teacher. So it is to you, dear colleague, that I leave the real job. What I have been trying to do here is to provide material that can open doors to meaningful and interesting language work. My approach combines the philosophies of "whole language" with humanistic, communicative methodologies. I believe that language, perhaps unlike other fields of cognitive endeavor, is learned more unsystematically than it is systematically. That is, we don't learn a language to use it. Rather, we learn a language while we are using it and we use language because we have messages to deliver and thoughts we want to express.

One of the best ways of learning anything is through a good story. Most religious teaching that has had a profound and influential effect on human activity has been taught through stories. A story speaks to us because it touches the narrative of our own lives. Thus, while we talk, think, and write about a story, we are really thinking, talking, and writing about ourselves.

The stories in *Stories with a Twist* are intended to open up the language abilities of English language learners. Such stories make students *want* to express themselves and reach for the right word or expression in order to tell their classmates important things about the way they see themselves, their world, and their lives.

## Organization of the Text

The organization of *Stories with a Twist* follows certain established routines. I have chosen such a structure because I think that classroom routines and frameworks make both students and teachers more comfortable and secure. Each unit contains the following sections:

- Before You Read
- The Story
- Thinking About the Story
- Working with Words
- Working with Language
- Asking Questions
- Rewriting the Story
- Retelling the Story
- Extending the Story

Once the patterns and frameworks have been established, the content of each routine can be endlessly varied and extended. *Stories with a Twist* suggests a number of variations. The rest is up to you. I know that classroom teachers are creative people who always put their own spin on things. No textbook should control you. You are the one who controls the textbook!

## Planning Lessons

*Stories with a Twist* is not a grammar book. If you use it as a main text with high beginning or low intermediate students, you might want a standard grammar book to accompany it and add the structure you need. The language points presented in *Stories with a Twist* are drawn from context and are meant to be worked on as acquired chunks of language. If students are working through a grammar book at the same time, they will have one of those "aha" moments when they reach the grammatical explanation of an already acquired chunk. I have included the "Working with Language" sections because I believe that language learning is a process that comes at the learner from many different directions. I feel that practicing a discrete language point that has appeared inside meaningful content can, indeed, be very useful.

Here is how I envision a typical two-hour lesson using *Stories with a Twist:*

1. Attract students' attention to the picture and comment on it.

2. Have students, in small groups, talk about the questions that relate to the picture.

3. Circulate, helping out with vocabulary and adding your own questions and suggestions.

4. Attract students' attention by creating a bridge sentence to the story. For example, in Story 3, *The Test,* you might say, "In the picture, the young man is writing a letter. How is letter writing different from writing email messages? (Get responses from the students.) This story is called *The Test.* I find this confusing. How do you think that writing letters is connected to taking tests? (Get responses.) Well, let's see just what happens as we read the story."

5. Read the story. Ask for choral reading and individual student readings when appropriate.

6. Read through the vocabulary list. Ask students to listen and repeat the words. Elicit meanings of the words from the students. Explain words when necessary.

7. Have students, in small groups, reread the story. Whenever there is dialogue in the story, have students practice it in pairs and/or present it to the class in individual pairs.

8. Have students, in small groups, discuss and do the comprehension exercises ("Thinking About the Story" section). Get students to switch groups after they finish the first exercise, so that they are working in a new group setting for the second exercise.

9. Have a break.

10. Ask students to do the "Working with Words," "Working with Language," and "Asking Questions" exercises.

11. Ask students to work on the rewriting exercise.

12. Check and comment on all the exercises.

13. Have students retell the story ("Retelling the Story" section).

14. Assign the exercises suggested in the "Extending the Story" section for the next lesson. For the second lesson, precede the central presentation with a review.

I have tried to give these stories an optimistic flavor and have attempted to create emotive links to the lives of the students. Such links, I have discovered, promote language learning. I hope that you enjoy the book. I would appreciate any comments and suggestions that you might be willing to pass along!

Sincerely,

Natalie Hess, Ph.D.
natalie.hess@nau.edu

## �֎ To the Student

WELCOME to *Stories with a Twist!* We've all experienced "twists" in life—when something other than what we expect happens. In these stories, the things that happen are close to things that happen in real life. I hope that you'll find meanings in these stories that encourage you to express important things about yourself, your life, and your world.

I also encourage you to write and tell me some of your thoughts about the stories and about the progress you are making in English. Enjoy these stories—and good luck with your studies!

Sincerely,

*Natalie Hess*

Natalie Hess, Ph.D.
natalie.hess@nau.edu

*Story 1*

# The Most Precious Diamonds

## ✵ Before You Read

*Talking About the Picture*

Look at the picture. Then, with a partner, answer the questions below. When you have finished talking to your partner, tell the rest of the class what you decided. Listen to the ideas of the other students.

- Who is the young woman in the picture?
- How old do you think she is?
- What do you think she does each day?
- What is she getting ready for?
- Do you think she is happy about what is going to happen?
- How and why do you think that the earrings are important to the young woman?

1

Knowing the words below will help you to understand the story. Listen and repeat as your teacher reads the words. Do you know what these words mean? Ask your teacher or your classmates to help you if you need a meaning explained. Then read the story.

| | | | |
|---|---|---|---|
| to expect | to borrow | to dare | to agree |
| to invite | earrings | to discover | skills |
| to remind | slender | mirror | fake |
| jewelry | expensive | jeweler | precious |
| jealous | | | |

## ❋ The Story

# *The Most Precious Diamonds*

SARAH HAD GROWN UP in a family that had a lot of money. Sarah lived in a large house that had a beautiful garden. When she was a small girl, she had everything she wanted— many toys, trips to interesting places, and beautiful clothes. She grew up expecting to get the best of everything all her life, but when Sarah was sixteen years old, her father lost all his money and the family became poor. Sarah had to work as a salesperson in a store, and she hated her work. She hated the cheap clothes she had to buy. She hated to get up early in the morning and hurry to work, and most of all she hated having to worry and think about money all the time.

Some of Sarah's friends from the time she was a little girl still invited her to parties. Sarah both loved and hated these parties. She loved the parties because they reminded her of the time she was rich and happy. But she also hated the parties because she never had the right clothes or the right jewelry to wear, and she was always very jealous of the people who had everything.

One day in December, Sarah's friend Jane, who had known Sarah as a little girl, invited Sarah to a big Christmas party. Sarah

2

wanted so much to go, but she just didn't have the right dress. 20
Luckily, Jane understood. She let Sarah borrow a beautiful green
dress and pulled a pair of diamond earrings from her jewelry box.

"Here, Sarah," she said, "these are perfect earrings for you.
They will frame your face beautifully and show off your slender
neck." 25

Sarah loved the dress, and she especially loved the earrings.
"Oh, Jane," she said, "these are so beautiful. I'd just love to wear
them, but I can see that they are real diamonds and very expensive.
I don't dare borrow them."

"Don't be silly," Jane said. "They'll look beautiful on you. 30
These diamonds were made for you. Just come and enjoy the
party."

And Sarah did. She danced the whole evening, and she felt
like a princess.

But when she got home, a terrible thing happened. When 35
she was undressing, she suddenly discovered that she had lost one of
the earrings. Poor Sarah! Poor Sarah! She just stood in front of the
mirror and cried. What was she going to tell her friend Jane?

The next day, Sarah went to see a jeweler with the one
earring she still had. 40

"Can you make me an earring with diamonds just like this
one?" she asked

"Yes," said the jeweler, "but it will cost you two
thousand four hundred dollars."

"Can I pay you one hundred dollars every month?" Sarah 45
asked.

The jeweler agreed, and the next day, Sarah returned the
earrings to her friend Jane. For two years, Sarah had to pay one
hundred dollars every single month. It was not easy because Sarah
earned only two hundred dollars a month. Soon Sarah decided that 50
she had better find a job that paid more. In the evenings after she
finished work in the store, Sarah went to school to learn new skills.
She had discovered that she was very good at cutting hair and
putting on makeup, so she became a beautician. Soon she had a

very enjoyable job, and she found that she loved her work and felt 55
really good about herself. She was working hard, but she was
earning her own money. Margaret, her boss, made Sarah a partner
in the business, and before the two years were up, Sarah had her
own shop. She didn't go to the rich people's parties any more. She
just didn't have time, but many of her friends from childhood came 60
to have their hair fixed in her shop. Sarah was proud of herself and
her shop. She was no longer jealous of anyone.

One day, Jane came into Sarah's shop. "Oh, Sarah," Jane said,
"you are so lucky to be independent. What a wonderful life you
have. I am proud to have you as a friend." 65

"But everything happened because of you," Sarah told her
friend.

"Because of me?" Jane was very surprised.

"Yes," Sarah told her. "I only became a beautician because I
had to pay for your earring." She explained everything to her friend. 70

"Oh, Sarah," Jane said, "I am so sorry. I should have told
you."

"Told me what?" Sarah asked.

"The earrings I lent you that night for the party were not
real diamonds. I never wear real jewelry. You were wearing fake 75
diamonds that night—maybe they were worth twenty dollars at the
most. I didn't tell you because you believed they were real and that
made you feel special. Oh, I am sorry, Sarah!"

But Sarah just laughed! "Oh, they were real diamonds for
me," she said. "They were the most precious diamonds in the 80
world!"

85

4

## ❋ Thinking About the Story

*What Did You Understand?*

A. Answer the following questions in complete sentences. Write your answers in the empty spaces. Then compare your answers with those of a classmate. Your teacher may wish to put these questions on the walls of your classroom and ask you to walk around with a partner answering the questions. Then each of you could take down one question and read it out loud so that the whole class can talk about it.

1. Why was Sarah unhappy?

   _____

2. How did one of Sarah's friends help out?

   _____

3. What happened during the party?

   _____

4. What happened after the party?

   _____

5. Why was it good that Sarah lost the earring?

   _____

6. What did Sarah mean when she said, "They were the most precious diamonds in the world"?

   _____

B. Correct the sentences below according to the content of the story. Write your corrections in the blanks and compare what you have written with a classmate.

1. Sarah had no reason to be jealous.

   _____

2. Sarah had no friends after her family lost their money.

   _____

3. Sarah didn't enjoy the party.

   _____

4. Sarah was not very worried when she discovered that she had lost one of the earrings.

   _____

5. The lost earring was not very important for Sarah.

   _____

C. Below is a list of possible names or titles for some of the paragraphs in the story. Match a paragraph with a name, and then compare your matches with those of several classmates.

Getting Ready
Love and Hate
Independence is Better than Jewelry
Something Terrible
A Big Change
The Jeweler
Paying Back
The Little Princess

# ✳ Working with Words

The words *remind* and *remember* are very often confused. We remember things that have happened to us; the opposite of *to remember* is *to forget*. We remind ourselves of other people or things that we or they might forget or have forgotten. For example, we might remind someone that he/she has to return a book to the library or that he/she has a dentist appointment. In the sentences below, use either *remind* or *remember* in an appropriate tense. Then compare your answers with those of a classmate.

1. My friend _____ me that I had to meet him at 3:00 in the library. I was glad that he _____ me because I had completely forgotten. It's not easy to _____ everything when you are in a new country.

2. I don't _____ anything that happened in San Francisco because I was so tired then. I am so glad that you _____ me of that wonderful Chinese restaurant. The next time I am in San Francisco, I must _____ to go there again.

3. Please _____ me that I have a doctor's appointment next week. I will be so busy that I just might not _____.

4. _____ the accident that happened when I was five years old? Please don't _____ me about it. If I don't have to think about it, I would rather not _____, but unfortunately, I do _____ all of the details.

5. He tries not to _____ anything about Vietnam. It was such a terrible experience for him, but when he visited Cambodia, suddenly everything _____ him of life in Vietnam during the war.

## ❋ Working with Language

Jane is sorry that she did not tell Sarah that the earrings were fake jewels. She says, "I should have told you!" We use *should have* and the third form (past participle) of the verb when we are sorry that we didn't do something that we should have done.

Think of three things you should have done recently that you didn't do. Write these three things in the blanks below. Then in small groups, tell your classmates about the things you should have done and listen to the things your classmates think they should have done.

I should have _____.

I should have _____.

I should have _____.

## ❋ Asking Questions

Following are answers to questions. Working with a partner, decide what the questions are. Write your questions in the blank spaces and compare your questions with those of other students.

1. _____?
   Answer: Her father lost all of his money.

2. _____?
   Answer: Sarah had to work as a salesperson in a store.

3. _____?
   Answer: She didn't have the right dress.

4. _____?
   Answer: She lost one of the earrings.

5. _____?
   Answer: She learned a new profession.

## ✳ Rewriting the Story

Below is the story you just read, only now words are missing from it. Some of the blanks need only one word in them. Others need several words. First, fill in as many of the missing words as you can on your own. Then, working with a classmate, fill in the rest of the blanks to make the story complete. Check this story with the complete story.

## *The Most Precious Diamonds*

SARAH HAD GROWN UP in a family that had 1. _____. Sarah lived in a large house that had a beautiful garden. When she was a small girl, she had everything she wanted—many toys, trips to interesting places, and beautiful clothes. She grew up expecting to get the best of everything all her 2. _____, but when Sarah was sixteen years old, her father lost all his money and the family became 3. _____. Sarah had to work as a salesperson in a store, and she hated her work. She hated the cheap clothes she had to buy. She hated to get up early in the morning and hurry to work, and most of all she hated having to worry and think about 4. _____ all the time.

Some of Sarah's friends from the time she was a little girl still invited her to their parties. Sarah both loved and 5. _____ these parties. She loved the parties because they reminded her of the time she was 6. _____ and happy. But she also hated the parties because she never had the right 7. _____ or the right jewelry to wear, and she was always very 8. _____ of the people who had everything.

One day in December, Sarah's friend Jane, who had known Sarah as a little girl, invited Sarah to a big 9. _____ party. Sarah wanted so much to go, but she just didn't have the right dress. Luckily, Jane understood. She let Sarah borrow a beautiful green dress and pulled a pair of 10. _____ earrings from her jewelry box.

9

"Here, Sarah," she said, "these are perfect earrings for you. They will frame your face beautifully and show off your slender neck."

Sarah loved the dress, and she especially loved the earrings. "Oh, Jane," she said, "these are so beautiful. I'd just love to wear them, but I can see that they are real 11. _____ and very 12. _____. I don't dare 13. _____ them."

"Don't be silly," Jane said. "They'll look beautiful on you. These diamonds were made for you. Just come and 14. _____ the party."

And Sarah did. She danced the whole evening, and she felt like a princess. But when she got home, a terrible thing happened. When she was undressing, she suddenly 15. _____ that she had lost one of the earrings. Poor Sarah! Poor Sarah! She just stood in front of the mirror and cried. What was she going to tell her friend Jane?

The next day, Sarah went to see a jeweler with the one earring she still had. "Can you make me an earring with diamonds just like this one?" she asked.

"Yes," said the jeweler, "but it will cost you two thousand four hundred dollars."

"Can I pay you one hundred dollars every 16. _____?" Sarah asked.

The jeweler agreed, and the next day, Sarah returned the earrings to her friend Jane. For two years, Sarah had to pay one hundred dollars every single month. It was not 17. _____ because Sarah only made two hundred dollars a month. Soon Sarah decided that she had better find a job that paid more. In the evenings after she finished work in the store, Sarah went to school to learn new 18. _____. She had discovered that she was very good at cutting hair and putting on make-up, so she became a beautician. Soon she had a very enjoyable job, and she found that she loved her work and felt really good about herself. She was working hard, but she was 19. _____ her own money. Margaret, her boss, made Sarah a 20. _____ in the business, and before the two years were up, Sarah had her own shop. She didn't go to the rich people's parties any more. She just didn't have time, but many of her friends from childhood came to have their hair fixed in her shop. Sarah was 21. _____ of herself and her shop. She was no longer 22. _____ of anyone.

One day, Jane came into Sarah's shop. "Oh, Sarah," Jane said. "you are so lucky to be 23. _____. What a wonderful life you have. I am proud to have you as a friend."

"But everything happened because of 24. _____," Sarah told her friend.

"Because of me?" Jane was very 25. _____.

"Yes," Sarah told her. "I only became a beautician because I had to pay for your earring." She explained everything to her friend.

"Oh, Sarah," Jane said, "I'm so sorry. I should have told you."

"Told me what?" Sarah asked.

"The earrings I lent you that night for the party were not 26. _____ diamonds. I never wear real jewelry. You were wearing 27. _____ diamonds that night—maybe they were worth twenty dollars at the most. I didn't tell you because you believed they were real and that made you feel 28. _____. Oh, I am so sorry, Sarah!"

But Sarah just laughed! "Oh, they were real diamonds for me," she said. "They were the most precious diamonds in the world!"

## ❋ Retelling the Story

Working with a classmate, tell each other the story in your own words. Use the following words and expressions to help you.

toys
beautiful clothes
lost his money
invited to parties
Christmas party
earrings
real diamonds
lost one of the earrings

jeweler
find a job
beautician
proud of herself
independent
fake jewelry
the most precious diamonds

## ❋ Extending the Story

A. In the story Sarah becomes happy after she becomes independent and loves her work. Different things make different people happy. On the next page is a list of things that might make people happy. Put the list in the right order for you. Put the thing that would make you happiest first and then continue the list. If there is something that makes you especially happy, but it is not on the list, add it to the list. Then, in groups of three, tell your classmates the order of your list and why you think that these things make you happy. Listen to what your classmates have to say.

| The Master List | My Own List |
|---|---|
| a good job | _____ |
| plenty of money | _____ |
| security | _____ |
| many friends | _____ |
| music | _____ |
| sports and exercise | _____ |
| entertainment | _____ |
| love | _____ |
| a good family | _____ |
| religion | _____ |
| spirituality | _____ |
| hobbies | _____ |
| a good social life | _____ |
| good health | _____ |
| helping other people | _____ |
| being famous | _____ |

B. In small groups, explain to your classmates why you agree or disagree with the sentences below.

I like casual clothes best.

Sometimes it's very important to dress formally.

You can lose your job if you don't dress right for it.

I wish people would not pay so much attention to clothes.

C. Sarah likes her work as a beautician because she feels good about earning her own money. She has earned self-respect and self-esteem. What other ways help a person earn self-respect? How important do you think self-esteem is to a person?

D. With a partner, complete the sentences below and act out the conversation between a salesperson in a large department store and a customer. Later, you and a classmate might want to act out your dialogue in front of the class.

**Salesperson:**    Hello, can I help you?

**Customer:**    Yes, please. I have to go to a _____ tomorrow, and I need _____ and _____.

**Salesperson:**    Good, we have just what you need. Please come this way.

*Story 2*

# The Guardian Angel

## ❋ Before You Read

*Talking About the Picture*

Look at the picture. Then, with a partner, answer the questions below. When you have finished talking to your partner, tell the rest of the class what you decided. Listen to the ideas of the other students.

- What is happening in the picture?
- What do you think happened just minutes before the action in the picture?
- What will be happening in the next few seconds and minutes?
- Do you think the man in the picture is related to the little girl?
- How do you think the title, *The Guardian Angel,* is connected to the story?

Knowing the words below will help you to understand the story. Listen and repeat as your teacher reads the words. Do you know what these words mean? Ask your teacher or your classmates to help you if you need a meaning explained. Then read the story.

| | | |
|---|---|---|
| stock market | owner | flames |
| my own fault | investment | hose |
| to blame | shoulder | scared |
| errand boy | guardian angel | dangerous |
| salesman | to crowd | kindly |
| manager | fire engine | |

## ❋ The Story

# *The Guardian Angel*

GILBERT BENSON was 35 years old and very sad. He was walking on the streets of New York with his head down. He walked and walked, not thinking about where he was going. Gilbert had lost all of his money in the stock market that morning, and he felt like his life was over. He was very depressed. He knew that the woman he was in love with would not want to marry him now.

"Yesterday I had many friends," Gilbert thought to himself. "But today I don't even have one friend. Yesterday the sun was shining in the sky, but today the sky is gray. The sun will never shine on me again. I'm finished. And it is my own fault. I have no one to blame but myself."

Gilbert was raised in a very poor family. When he was sixteen years old, he started working in a shoe store. First he was an errand boy, then a salesman, then a manager, then a part-owner, then the owner of one shoe store, then the owner of two shoe stores, and finally the owner of three shoe stores. Life was good for him, but Gilbert was tired of working so hard. He wanted to get rich fast, so he decided to invest his money. He made a bad investment, however, and lost everything he had worked so hard for—his money and his shoe stores were gone forever.

Gilbert walked and walked, not looking where he was going. He started to cross a street when suddenly he felt a hand grab his shoulder and pull him back. A car rushed past him. It all happened quickly, and Gilbert realized that the light was flashing "don't walk." If he had walked out into the street, he would have been hit and possibly killed by the car. "I wish that I had been killed," Gilbert thought. He looked around to see who had stopped him from crossing the street, but no one was there. "I guess that was my guardian angel," Gilbert said to himself. Then he laughed out loud because he didn't believe in guardian angels.

Gilbert continued to walk. He still felt bad and sorry for himself, and he kept thinking how his life could've ended just minutes ago. He thought about the car hitting him, and then he started thinking about other ways to hurt himself. No one would care—he didn't have any friends, and his girlfriend would only love him if he had money.

Then from far away, Gilbert heard the loud sound of sirens. "Someone else is hurt," he thought, and he wished it were him. The sound got louder and louder, and soon a fire engine rushed past Gilbert. Many people saw the fire engine and started running after it. Gilbert decided to follow them. At the end of the street there was a huge house on fire. The people crowded around the house while policemen tried to keep them back. One woman was screaming through the crowd, "Lucy! Lucy! My child is still in the house. Help! I have to get inside and save Lucy!" She pushed through the crowd, scared and worried. A policeman grabbed her. "You can't go in there now," he shouted. "The flames are up to the third floor, and it's very dangerous."

"You don't understand!" The woman shouted, "It's Lucy, my daughter. I can't live without Lucy. She's in the house. Please help!"

Suddenly Gilbert understood. He realized how scared and sad the woman must feel, and he knew he needed to help her. He ran behind the house. There, in a window on the third floor, he saw

Lucy. She was holding a blanket and crying. People were shouting 55
all kinds of things to her, but she didn't move. Gilbert came closer
to the house. The flames were getting bigger and bigger behind the
little girl. Then her eyes met his. He reached out his arms for her,
motioning that he would catch her. The little girl let go of her
blanket and jumped. He caught her just as the window began to 60
burn. The little girl held him with all her strength. Suddenly,
Gilbert felt like a very different person.

Gilbert walked home that afternoon with his head up. He
was no longer thinking about all the money he had lost. He wasn't
thinking that maybe his girlfriend wouldn't love him anymore, or 65
how he wanted to die. The afternoon sun still seemed bright, and as
Gilbert stopped at a street corner, he felt something like a hand
touch him kindly on his back as the light turned green.

## ❈ Thinking About the Story

*What Did You Understand?*

A. Answer the following questions in complete sentences. Write
your answers in the empty spaces. Then compare your answers
with those of a classmate. Your teacher may wish to put these
questions on the walls of your classroom and ask you to walk
around with a partner answering the questions. Then each
of you could take down one question and read it out loud, so
that the whole class can talk about it.

1. Why is Gilbert so depressed? (Give several reasons.)

_____

2. How had Gilbert made his money?

_____

3. What makes Gilbert suddenly laugh?

_____

4. Why does Gilbert follow the people?

_____

5. In what way is Gilbert's behavior different from that of the other people at the scene of the fire?

_____

_____

6. Why does Gilbert feel like a different person?

_____

_____

7. What do you think might happen to Gilbert in the next weeks? Months? Years?

_____

_____

B. Correct the sentences below according to the content of the story. Write your corrections in the blanks and compare what you have written with a classmate.

1. Gilbert came from a rich family.

_____

2. Gilbert blamed other people for his problems.

_____

3. Gilbert never made a foolish decision.

_____

4. Gilbert believed in the power of angels.

_____

5. Gilbert will always think that money is the most important thing in the world.

_____

_____

## ❊ Working with Words

Finish the sentences below in any way you want. Then read your sentences to a classmate and listen to his/her sentences.

1. It is important to know how to support yourself because

_____.

2. I don't like to blame other people when

_____.

3. A good salesperson must

_____.

4. The flames were high, and I was afraid that

_____.

5. Today my shoulder hurts because

_____.

## ✳ Working with Language

When a car almost hits him, Gilbert says, "I wish that I had been killed."

After the word *wish,* we use the past tense. We say "I wish it would rain" or "I wish I could swim." In the spaces below write three wishes for yourself. Then tell two classmates about your wishes and listen to their wishes. Perhaps your wishes will come true!

*My Three Wishes*

1. _____
2. _____
3. _____

## ✳ Asking Questions

Following are answers to questions. Working with a partner, decide what the questions are. Write your questions in the blank spaces and compare your questions with those of other students.

1. _____?
   Answer: Because he had lost all his money, and he was sure that he had no friends.

2. _____?
   Answer: He had made a bad investment.

3. _____?
   Answer: He was an errand boy.

4. _____?
   Answer: He had lost his money and three shoe stores.

5. _____?
   Answer: Because the little girl trusted him.

## ❋ Rewriting the Story

Below is the story you just read, only now words are missing from it. Some of the blanks need only one word in them. Others need several words. First, fill in as many of the missing words as you can on your own. Then, working with a classmate, fill in the rest of the blanks to make the story complete. Check this story with the complete story.

# The Guardian Angel

G ILBERT BENSON was 35 years old and very sad. He was walking on the streets of New York with his head down. He walked and walked, not thinking about where he was 1. _____. Gilbert had lost all of his money in the stock market that morning, and he felt like his life 2. _____. He was very depressed. He knew that the woman he was 3. _____ would not want to marry him now.

"Yesterday I had many friends," Gilbert thought to himself. "But today I don't even have one 4. _____. Yesterday the sun was shining in the sky, but today the sky is gray. The sun will never shine on me again. I'm finished. And it is my own 5. _____. I have no one to blame but myself."

Gilbert was raised in a very 6. _____ family. When he was sixteen years old, he started 7. _____ in a shoe store. First he was an errand boy, then a 8. _____, then a manager, then a part-owner, then the owner of one shoe store, then the owner of two shoe stores, and finally the owner of three shoe stores. Life was good for him, but Gilbert was 9. _____ of working so hard. He wanted to get rich fast, so he decided to invest his money. He made a bad 10. _____, however, and lost everything he had worked so hard for—his money and his 11. _____ were gone forever.

Gilbert walked and walked, not looking where he was going. He started to cross a street when suddenly he felt a hand grab his 12. _____ and pull him back. A car rushed past him. It all happened quickly, and Gilbert realized that the light was 13. _____ "don't walk." If he had walked out into the street, he 14. _____ hit and possibly killed by the car. "I wish that I had been killed," Gilbert thought. He looked around to see who had stopped him from crossing the street, but 15. _____ was there. "I guess that was my guardian angel," Gilbert said to himself. Then he laughed out loud because he didn't 16. _____ in guardian angels.

Gilbert continued to walk. He still felt bad and sorry for himself, and he kept thinking how his life could've 17. _____ just minutes ago. He thought about the car hitting him, and then he started thinking about other ways to hurt 18. _____. No one would care—he 19. _____ any friends, and his girlfriend would only love him if he had 20. _____.

Then from far away, Gilbert heard the loud sound of sirens. "Someone else is hurt," he thought, and he wished it were him. The sound got louder and louder, and soon a 21. _____ rushed past Gilbert. Many people saw the fire engine and 22. _____ after it. Gilbert decided to follow them. At the end of the street there was a huge house on 23. _____. The people crowded around the house while policemen tried to keep them back. One woman was screaming through the crowd, "Lucy! Lucy! My child is still in the house. Help! I have to get 24. _____ and save Lucy!" She pushed through the crowd, scared and worried. A policeman grabbed her. "You can't go in there now," he shouted. "The flames are up to the third floor, and it's very 25. _____."

"You don't understand!" The woman shouted, "It's Lucy, my daughter. I can't live without Lucy. She's in the house. Please help!"

Suddenly Gilbert understood. He realized how scared and sad the woman must feel, and he knew he needed to help her. He ran 26. _____ the house. There, in a window on the third floor, he saw Lucy. She was holding a blanket and crying. People were shouting all kinds of things to her, but she didn't 27. _____. Gilbert came closer to the house. The flames were getting bigger and bigger behind the little girl. Then her eyes met his. He 28. _____ his arms for her, motioning that he would catch her. The little girl let go of her blanket and jumped. He caught her just as the window began to burn. The little girl held him with all her strength. Suddenly, Gilbert felt like a very 29. _____ person.

Gilbert walked home that afternoon with his head up. He was no longer thinking about all the money he 30. _____. He wasn't thinking that maybe his girlfriend wouldn't love him anymore, or how he wanted 31. _____. The afternoon sun still seemed bright, and as Gilbert stopped at a street corner, he felt something like a 32. _____ touch him kindly on his back as the light turned green.

## ✻ Retelling the Story

Working with a classmate, tell each other the story in your own words. Use the following words and expressions to help you.

| | |
|---|---|
| head down | fire engine |
| blame myself | flames |
| poor family | third floor |
| wanted to get rich | little girl |
| bad investment | jump |
| shoulder | different person |
| no one there | touch him |

## ✻ Extending the Story

A. A newspaper reporter comes to interview Gilbert about having saved Lucy from the fire. In small groups, decide what kinds of questions the reporter might ask. Then, in pairs, act out the interview.

B. Write a short newspaper story about Gilbert and the fire. Remember to give your article a headline. Your teacher might talk to you about how headline language is special.

# The Test

## ❋ Before You Read

*Talking About the Picture*

Look at the picture. Then, with a partner, answer the questions below. When you have finished talking to your partner, tell the rest of the class what you decided. Listen to the ideas of the other students.

- Do you like to get letters?
- Do you write to many people?
- Have you ever met any one through email or through the Internet?
- Do you think that this is a good way to meet people?
- How is writing letters different from talking face-to-face with someone?
- The name of the story is *The Test*. How do you think that letter writing is connected to tests?

*Previewing the Vocabulary*

Knowing the words below will help you to understand the story. Listen and repeat as your teacher reads the words. Do you know what these words mean? Ask your teacher or your classmates to help you if you need a meaning explained. Then read the story.

| | | |
|---|---|---|
| poems | recognize | excited |
| to imagine | disappointed | to introduce |
| fought | expensive | drug store |
| to enjoy | wrinkles | |

## ❋ The Story

### The Test

CHARLIE WAS A STUDENT at the University of Indiana. He studied hard and often went to the library to read books. One day he found a book of poems. Its pages were torn, and in the white spaces by the poems there were notes written in pencil. Charlie enjoyed reading the poems, but more than anything, he enjoyed reading the notes written in pencil by the poems. The person who wrote them seemed very smart, and the writing was perfect. Charlie wished he knew the person; even just to see what the person looked like. He imagined the person to be very good-looking, just like the writing. Then one day, on one of the last pages of the book, Charlie found a note with a name under it. The name was "Stella Richardson." "Maybe this is the name of the person who has written all these wonderful things in pencil," Charlie thought. He looked up the name "Stella Richardson" in the student directory.

It took Charlie a few weeks to find out information about Stella. He had to ask many people and go many places. Stella was no longer a student at the university. He found out that she had moved to New York, and when he got her address, he wrote her a

28

long letter. Stella wrote him back. Her writing was even more <sup></sup> beautiful than her notes in the book of poems. Soon, Charlie was writing Stella once a week, and through letters they learned many things about each other. Charlie felt like he had known Stella forever. He couldn't wait to meet Stella and he decided that he would take a trip to New York to see her. [25]

But Charlie's plans quickly changed. World War II had started, and Charlie was sent away with the army. He was sent to France, where he lived and fought as a soldier for three years.

It was difficult and expensive to send letters from France, but for three years Charlie and Stella continued to write each other. [30] In his letters, Charlie told Stella everything that was happening to him, and Stella wrote back wonderful letters that helped Charlie make it through the war. When the war was over, Charlie wrote Stella to tell her that he was coming home. The army was sending him through New York, and he hoped he could meet Stella at the [35] train station. Stella wrote that she would be wearing a red rose in her hair so Charlie could recognize her.

Charlie dreamed of red roses on his way back from France. He was so excited. Finally, he would meet the person who he felt was his best friend. When Charlie got off the train in New York, he [40] saw a young woman with lovely green eyes and thick, curly brown hair. He thought she was beautiful, and he wished she were Stella, but there was no red rose in her hair. Charlie looked and looked at all the people in the station. Finally, he saw an elderly woman standing alone. There were wrinkles across her face, and her hair [45] was gray like the color of the train. She looked up at Charlie, and then Charlie noticed a red rose.

Poor Charlie felt very sad and disappointed. This was not the woman he dreamed about. But this was the woman who, for many years, never stopped writing him such wonderful letters. Charlie [50] knew that he loved the way she wrote. He loved the way she thought about things, and he decided that she could be a good friend to him, even if she wasn't what he had imagined.

Charlie walked up to the woman and introduced himself. "Hello," he said. "I'm Charlie, and you must be Stella. May I take you out to dinner?"

The elderly woman smiled. "You seem like a very nice young man," she said, "But I am not Stella, and I don't quite understand what this is all about. A young woman just walked by and asked me to put this rose in my hair. She told me that if someone named Charlie asked me out to dinner, I should tell him that Stella is waiting for him in the corner drugstore. She said that it was an important test."

And so Charlie had passed the test of a lifetime—the test of love!

## ✳ Thinking About the Story

### *What Did You Understand?*

A. Answer the following questions in complete sentences. Write your answers in the empty spaces. Then compare your answers with those of a classmate. Your teacher may wish to put these questions on the walls of your classroom and ask you to walk around with a partner answering the questions. Then each of you could take down one question and read it out loud, so that the whole class can talk about it.

1. Why did Charlie start writing to Stella?

_____

2. Why didn't Charlie go to New York the first time?

_____

3. What happened when Charlie went to Europe?

_____

4. What happened after the war?

_____

5. Who was the first person Charlie saw at the train station?

_____

6. Who had a red rose in her hair?

_____

7. Why was the test important to Stella?

_____

B. Correct the sentences below according to the content of the story. Write your corrections in the blanks and compare what you have written with a classmate.

1. Charlie and Stella met in the library.

_____

2. Charlie fell in love with Stella because he loved the way she looked.

_____

3. When Charlie went to Europe, Charlie and Stella stopped writing to each other.

_____

_____

4. Stella wanted Charlie to like the elderly woman.

_____

5. Stella didn't want to meet Charlie.

_____

## ✸ Working with Words

*Excited, sad,* and *disappointed* are all words that express how we feel about things. Complete the sentences below in different ways. Think of three things that make you feel excited, sad, or disappointed about something. Then compare your sentences with those of a classmate.

I feel excited when

_____

_____

_____.

I feel sad when

_____

_____

_____.

I feel disappointed when

_____

_____

_____.

## ✸ Working with Language

Charlie looked up Stella's name in the student directory. In this sentence *look up* means to find something in a book. The word *look* changes its meanings when one adds different prepositions to it. *Look up* can mean simply to turn one's eyes toward the sky, and it can also mean something entirely different. For example, in the sentence "I look up to my father," *look up to* means "respect."

Using your dictionary, find meanings for the following phrases:

look down on someone _____

look through something _____

look over something _____

overlook something          _____

look up someone            _____

look up to someone         _____

look into something        _____

## ❋ Asking Questions

Following are answers to questions. Working with a partner, decide what the questions are. Write your questions in the blank spaces and compare your questions with those of other students.

1. _____?
   Answer: Through letters.

2. _____?
   Answer: In a book of poems.

3. _____?
   Answer: He had to ask many people.

4. _____?
   Answer: She lived in New York.

5. _____?
   Answer: He had to go to France.

## ❋ Rewriting the Story

Following is the story you just read, only now words are missing from it. Some of the blanks need only one word in them. Others need several words. First, fill in as many of the missing words as you can on your own. Then, working with a classmate, fill in the rest of the blanks to make the story complete. Check this story with the complete story.

# The Test

CHARLIE WAS A 1. _____ at the University of Indiana. He studied hard and often went to the library to read books. One day he found a 2. _____. Its pages were torn, and in the white spaces by the poems there were notes written in 3. _____. Charlie enjoyed reading the poems, but more than anything, he enjoyed reading the notes written in pencil by the poems. The person who wrote them seemed very smart, and the writing was perfect. Charlie 4. _____ he knew the person; even just to see what the person looked like. He 5. _____ the person to be very good-looking, just like the writing. Then one day, on one of the last pages of the book, Charlie found a note with a name under it. The name was "Stella Richardson." "Maybe this is the name of the person who has written all these wonderful things in pencil," Charlie thought. He 6. _____ the name "Stella Richardson" in the student directory.

It took Charlie a few weeks to find out information about Stella. He had to ask many people and go many places. Stella was no longer a student at the university. He found out that she 7. _____ to New York, and when he got her address, he wrote her a long 8. _____ Stella wrote him back. Her writing was even more beautiful than her notes in the book of poems. Soon, Charlie was writing Stella once a week, and through letters they learned many things about each other. Charlie felt like he had known Stella 9. _____. He couldn't wait to meet Stella and he decided that he would take a 10. _____ to New York to see her.

But Charlie's plans quickly 11. _____. World War II had started, and Charlie was sent away with the army. He was sent to France, where he lived and 12. _____ as a soldier for three years.

It was difficult and 13. _____ to send letters from France, but for three years Charlie and Stella continued to write each other. In his letters, Charlie told Stella everything that was happening to him, and Stella wrote back wonderful letters that helped Charlie make it through the war. When the war was over, Charlie wrote Stella to tell her that he was 14. _____. The army was sending him through New York, and he hoped he could meet Stella at the train station. Stella wrote that she would be wearing a 15. _____ in her hair so Charlie could recognize her.

Charlie dreamed of red roses on his way back from France. He was so excited. Finally, he would to meet the person who he felt was his best friend. When Charlie got off the train in New York, he saw a young woman with lovely green eyes and thick, curly brown hair. He thought she was 16. _____, and he wished she were Stella, but there was no red rose in her hair. Charlie looked and looked at all the people in the station. Finally he saw an 17. _____ woman standing alone. There were 18. _____ across her face, and her hair was gray like the color of the train. She looked up at Charlie, and then Charlie noticed a red rose.

Poor Charlie felt very sad and 19. _____. This was not the woman he 20. _____ about. But this was the woman who, for many years, never stopped writing him such wonderful letters. Charlie knew that he loved the way she wrote. He loved the way she thought about things, and he decided that she could be a 21. _____ to him, even if she wasn't what he had imagined.

Charlie walked up to the woman and 22. _____ himself. "Hello," he said. "I'm Charlie, and you must be Stella. May I take you out to dinner?"

The elderly woman 23. _____. "You seem like a very nice young man," she said, "But I am not Stella, and I don't quite understand what this is all about. A young woman just walked by and asked me to put this rose in my 24. _____. She told me that if someone named Charlie asked me out to 25. _____, I should tell him that Stella is waiting for him in the corner drugstore. She said that it was an important test."

And so Charlie had passed the 26. _____ of a lifetime—the test of love!

## ❋ Retelling the Story

Below are some words and expressions from the story. Work with a classmate and try to tell each other the story by using the words and expressions to help you.

| | |
|---|---|
| library | letters |
| book of poems | coming home |
| notes | rose |
| Stella | train |
| New York | young woman |
| war | elderly woman |
| France | disappointed |
| difficult | passed the test |

## ❋ Extending the Story

A. What is important when you choose a partner for life? On the next page is a list of things that many people consider important. Arrange the list in the order of importance to you. In the blank that says *Other* you can put in qualities that are not on the list. Then, in groups of three, tell your classmates the order of your list and explain why you have decided on this order.

My partner should be good looking.
My partner should be rich.
My partner should be very much like me.
My partner should be smart.
My partner must be kind.
My partner must be generous.
My partner should be sensible.

Other _____

*My Own List*

_____

_____

_____

_____

_____

_____

_____

B. Do you think that tests are important? In small groups, explain your thoughts about tests to your classmates. Tell your group about one important test in your life, and listen to what your classmates have to say. If someone in your group has talked about an interesting test, tell the rest of your class about it. Your teacher may ask you to write about the topic of tests for homework.

Story 4

# A Man with the Right Attitude

## ✷ Before You Read

*Talking About the Picture*

Look at the picture. Then, with a partner, answer the questions below. When you have finished talking to your partner, tell the rest of the class what you decided. Listen to the ideas of the other students.

- Where is this picture happening?
- Who are the people in the picture?
- What do you think happened right before this picture?
- What do you think will happen right after this picture?
- Why do you think the man in the picture is smiling?
- Why do you think that the man's attitude might be important?

Knowing the words below will help you to understand the story. Listen and repeat as your teacher reads the words. Do you know what these words mean? Ask your teacher or your classmates to help you if you need a meaning explained. Then read the story.

| | | |
|---|---|---|
| cheerful | to bleed | to operate |
| to choose | ambulance | allergic |
| choice | hospital | bullet |
| attitude | pale | jokes |
| to be held up | emergency room | |

## ❋ The Story

# *A Man with the Right Attitude*

**M**Y FRIEND LARRY is the happiest person I know. I have learned a lot from him. He is always cheerful. He is always in a good mood. He always has a smile on his face, and he always sees the good side of everyone. "Larry," I once asked him, "how can you be so happy?"                                          5

"It's easy," Larry said. "I choose to be happy. Every morning when I wake up I say to myself, 'Larry, you have a choice today. You can be happy or unhappy. You must choose," and then I choose to be happy."

Then something terrible happened to Larry, and I thought          10
his wonderful attitude would change.

One day two robbers held up Larry in a dark street. They took all his money and then shot him. The bullet went deep into Larry's stomach. For a very long time he lay in the street bleeding. Luckily, a woman who lived on the street saw that something was          15
wrong. She called an ambulance and Larry was rushed to a big hospital. When the nurses and doctors saw Larry's pale and bloody body in the emergency room, they grew worried. Larry had lost a

lot of blood, and there was a very small chance that he would live. The doctors were sad and serious as they wheeled Larry into the operating room. Larry knew that they had given up hope for him. He could see it in their faces and hear it in the way they talked quietly to each other. He knew that he had to do something fast to change their attitudes. 20

So, when a nurse asked Larry if he was allergic to anything, he shouted, "Yes!" The group of doctors and nurses stopped what they were doing. The room was silent. Everyone was listening. 25

"What is it?" asked one of the doctors, sounding even more worried than before. "What are you allergic to?"

Larry smiled. "I am allergic to bullets, so you better get this bullet out of me!" All of the doctors and nurses started to laugh. They realized that Larry was still very much alive and could make jokes even though he was hurt. Everyone felt better. Larry lived because he had chosen to be happy! He was still the man with the right attitude, and his attitude saved his life! 30 35

## ❋ Thinking About the Story

*What Did You Understand?*

Answer the following questions in complete sentences. Write your answers in the empty spaces. Then compare your answers with those of a classmate. Your teacher may wish to put these questions on the walls of your classroom and ask you to walk around with a partner answering the questions. Then each of you could take down one question and read it out loud, so that the whole class can talk about it.

1. What kind of a man was Larry?

_____

2. Why was Larry always cheerful?

_____

3. What happened to Larry one day?

_____

4. Why was Larry lucky?

_____

5. What happened in the hospital?

_____

6. Why did the doctors and nurses look so serious?

_____

7. Why did Larry make a decision?

_____

8. What can we learn from Larry?

_____

## ✸ Working with Words

Look at the two crossword puzzles. Person A has all the words going down. Person B has all the words across. Arrange your chairs in such a way that you sit with your back to your partner. Take turns giving each other definitions of the words. Try to give as many hints as possible to help your partner get the right word. When you have finished the puzzle, look it over together, and then check your answers with the completed puzzle on page 186.

# The Attitude Puzzle

## *Down*

1. the thing that is fired out of a gun
2. verb form of blood
3. the feelings you show
4. place for patients who have not made an appointment

# The Attitude Puzzle

## *Across*

3. the car that takes you to the hospital
5. puts on a happy face
6. sensitive to something
7. decide what is best
8. the opposite of wonderful
9. the noun of choose

# ✳ Working with Language

A nurse asked Larry if he was allergic to anything.

The nurse is asking an indirect question. If she had asked a direct question she would have said, "Larry, are you allergic to anything?"

Notice what happens when we change from a direct question to an indirect question:

We get rid of the quotation marks.

We go from present tense to past tense.

We put in the word *if.*

Working with a partner, change all the direct questions in Column A into indirect questions in Column B. Then compare your answers with the answers of the other students.

| Column A<br>*Direct Questions* | Column B<br>*Indirect Questions* |
|---|---|
| The doctor asked, "Do you feel all right?" | The doctor asked if_____<br>_____. |
| The nurse asked, "Are you allergic to anything?" | The nurse asked if_____<br>_____. |
| I said, "Larry, why are you always happy?" | I asked Larry why_____<br>_____. |
| Larry asked, "Does a person have a choice?" | Larry asked if _____<br>_____. |
| Larry asked, "Are you happy every day?" | Larry asked if _____<br>_____. |
| I asked, "Will Larry live?" | I asked if _____<br>_____. |

# ❋ Asking Questions

A. Following are answers to questions. Working with a partner, decide what the questions are. Write your questions in the blank spaces, and compare your questions with those of other students.

1. _____?
   Answer: I choose to be happy.

2. _____?
   Answer: Two robbers held up Larry.

3. _____?
   Answer: Yes, I am allergic to something.

4. _____?
   Answer: I am allergic to bullets.

5. _____?
   Answer: Because he had chosen to live.

B. It is important to know what kinds of questions a doctor or a nurse might ask you. One of them is, "Are you allergic to anything?"

Together with your teacher and classmates, make up other questions a doctor or nurse might ask new patients. In the spaces below, write down three such questions. Then together with a classmate, practice asking and answering the questions.

1. _____?

2. _____?

3. _____?

## ✳ Rewriting the Story

Below is the story you just read, only now words are missing from it. Some of the blanks need only one word in them. Others need several words. First, fill in as many of the missing words as you can on your own. Then, working with a classmate, fill in the rest of the blanks to make the story complete. Check this story with the complete story.

## *A Man with the Right* 1. _____

M Y FRIEND LARRY is the happiest person I know. I have learned a lot from him. He is always 2. _____. He is always in a 3. _____. He always has a smile on his face, and he always sees the 4. _____ of everyone. "Larry," I once asked him, "how can you be so happy?"

"It's easy," Larry said. "I 5. _____ to be happy. Every morning when I wake up I say to myself, 'Larry, you have a 6. _____ today. You can be happy or unhappy. You must choose," and then I choose to be 7. _____."

Then something 8. _____ happened to Larry, and I thought his wonderful attitude would change.

One day two robbers 9. _____ Larry in a dark street. They took all his money and then shot him. The bullet went deep into Larry's 10. _____. For a very long time he lay in the street 11. _____. Luckily, a woman who lived on the street saw that something was wrong. She called an 12. _____ and Larry was rushed to a big hospital. When the nurses and doctors saw Larry's pale and bloody body in the emergency room, they grew 13. _____. Larry had lost a lot of blood, and there was a very small chance that he would live. The doctors were sad and serious as they wheeled Larry into the 14. _____. Larry knew that they had given up 15. _____ for him. He could see it in their faces and hear it in the way the talked quietly to each

47

other. He knew that he had to do something fast to 16. _____ their attitudes.

So, when a 17. _____ asked Larry if he was 18. _____ to anything, he shouted, "Yes!" The group of doctors and nurses stopped what they were doing. The room was silent. Everyone was listening.

"What is it?" asked one of the doctors, sounding even more worried than before. "What are you allergic to?"

Larry smiled. "I am allergic to 19. _____, so you better get this bullet out of me!" All of the doctors and nurses started 20. _____. They realized that Larry was still very much alive and could make 21. _____ even though he was hurt. Everyone felt better. Larry lived because he had chosen to be happy! He was still the man with the right attitude, and his attitude saved his life!

## ✱ Retelling the Story

Working with a classmate, tell each other the story in your own words. Use the following words and expressions to help you.

| | |
|---|---|
| my friend Larry | hospital |
| happiest person | emergency room |
| cheerful | doctors and nurses |
| good mood | sad and serious |
| choose | attitude |
| something terrible | allergic |
| was held up | bullet |
| bleeding | joke |
| a woman | lived |
| ambulance | |

# ✽ Extending the Story

A. In the story Larry was seriously hurt. In our lives, we often have many small aches and pains.

Here are the names of our aches: (Notice that *ache* is pronounced like the end of the word *cake.)*

|            |              |
|------------|--------------|
| headache   | toothache    |
| backache   | side ache    |
| earache    | stomachache  |

For other parts of the body, we use the word *sore:*

|                 |                    |
|-----------------|--------------------|
| a sore eye      | sore legs          |
| a sore neck     | a sore foot        |
| a sore finger   | a sore muscle      |
| a sore mouth    | a sore throat      |
| sore lips       | a sore shoulder    |

Your teacher or one of your classmates will ask you "What's the matter?"
Pick one of the aches above or say what feels sore. Answer by saying "I have a _____."
Stand up and mingle. Ask other students "What's the matter?" and listen to them explain their ache. Then say "I'm sorry," and move on. When someone asks you "What's the matter?" tell that person what kind of ache you have or what is sore. Listen to him/her tell you that he/she is sorry.

B. Here is a conversation between someone calling for an appointment and a receptionist at a doctor's office. Listen to your teacher read the dialogue and repeat after him/her. Then practice the dialogue in pairs. Finally, change parts of the dialogue to make it your own. Use your own name and change anything else to suit you. Some of the students can act out their dialogues in front of the whole class.

| | |
|---|---|
| **Receptionist:** | Good Morning. Dr. Brown's office. |
| **Patient:** | I want to make an appointment with Dr. Brown. |
| **Receptionist:** | What's the matter? |
| **Patient:** | I have a terrible headache. |
| **Receptionist:** | I'm sorry. We have a free slot tomorrow at 10:00 a.m. Can you come then? |
| **Patient:** | Yes, I can. Thank you. |
| **Receptionist:** | What is your name? |
| **Patient:** | Suzanne Martin. |
| **Receptionist:** | Can you please spell that for me? |
| **Patient:** | Yes, that is S-U-Z-A-N-N-E Martin, M-A-R-T-I-N. |
| **Receptionist:** | Thank you, Ms. Martin. See you tomorrow at ten. |

C. In small groups, talk about the questions below. Ask one person in your group to write down some of the things you say. When you are finished, tell the whole class about what you said. Then listen to what the other groups have to say.

1. Can you really decide to be in a good mood? Why or why not?

2. Doctors say that people who are cheerful are healthier. Why do you think they are right?

3. Do you think that Larry saved his own life by telling a joke? Why or why not?

Story 5

# The Artist

## ✸ Before You Read

*Talking About the Picture*

Look at the picture. Then, with a partner, answer the questions below. When you have finished talking to your partner, tell the rest of the class what you decided. Listen to the ideas of the other students.

- What is happening in this picture?
- Do crimes like this happen in your country?
- Why do you think people commit crimes?
- What can be done to prevent such crimes?
- What is the best thing to do if you are caught in a situation like the one in the picture?

Knowing the words below will help you to understand the story. Listen and repeat as your teacher reads the words. Do you know what these words mean? Ask your teacher or your classmates to help you if you need a meaning explained. Then read the story.

| | | |
|---|---|---|
| directing traffic | sobs | to describe |
| a medal | mustache | exactly |
| to rob a bank | amazed | photographer |
| mayor | drugs | criminals |
| barely | grocery | missing persons |
| bruise | to remember | |

## ❈ The Story

## *The Artist*

**A**NTHONY FLORES was a very good policeman. He had worked at the Ludville Police Department for ten years and everyone in Ludville liked him. Anthony enjoyed his work. He liked to do everything from directing traffic to stopping crimes. He often went to schools and talked to children about how to be safe on the streets or about the dangers of using drugs. Twice, Anthony had caught criminals who tried to rob a bank in town. He also caught three adults who were trying to sell drugs to teenagers in the school parking lot. Because of all the good things Anthony did, the mayor of Ludville gave him a medal. Anthony seemed to have the life that everyone dreamed about.

But Anthony wasn't happy. He liked to help others, but being a policeman was not what Anthony really wanted to do. All his life, Anthony dreamed about being an artist. He loved to draw. In high school, he had drawn pictures of all kinds of people, from farmers to movie stars. He had drawn a picture of his parents sitting by the fire and drawn a picture of his girlfriend, Diana, feeding her horse. All of Anthony's pictures looked just like the people he painted, and in high school Anthony won many prizes for his wonderful artwork.

But now Anthony didn't have time to draw pictures. Being a policeman took a lot of hard work. At the end of the day, Anthony was always too tired to be an artist. Because Anthony couldn't be a policeman and an artist at the same time, he was very unhappy.

One day Mrs. Edna Lewis, the owner of the largest grocery store in Ludville, came running into the police station. She was crying, her dress was torn, and there was a huge bruise on her face. Anthony brought Edna a cup of coffee and calmly said, "Please, Edna, tell me what has happened."

Edna was so frightened and upset that she could barely talk. "Two men with guns came into the store—" She couldn't finish her sentence. She started crying again.

"Please, Edna," said Anthony. "I can't help you if you don't tell me what happened."

So, between sobs, Edna explained how the men had made everyone in the store lie down on the floor while one man pointed his gun at her. The men demanded that she give them all of the money in the cash register. Then one of them hit her across the face. He pushed her down and both men ran out of the store.

"Do you remember what the men looked like?" Anthony asked Edna.

"I—I think so," Edna said, "One had a mustache and big—"

"Wait a minute," Anthony interrupted. He went to his desk and came back with a notepad and a pencil. As Edna talked, Anthony began to draw. He drew every detail that Edna could remember. When Edna was finished describing the men, Anthony showed her his drawings. Edna was amazed.

"I can't believe it!" she said. "These pictures look exactly like those men. You are a real artist, Anthony—even better than a photographer!"

Anthony made copies of his pictures and posted them all over Ludville. Three days later, a woman recognized the criminals and helped the police find them.

But that was only the beginning for Anthony. Suddenly everyone wanted Anthony to draw pictures to help them. There were other store owners who had been robbed, families with missing children, and even people who had lost their pets. Anthony was drawing dozens of pictures every day from the descriptions people gave him. His drawings were very helpful to the Ludville police. Before long, Anthony got a job in the big city as a police artist. He moved to the city and took all of his paints, pencils, and paper with him. Now Anthony draws more people and things than he ever imagined. When Anthony goes home at night, he is still tired, but he is smiling, for he is living (and drawing) his dream.

## ❋ Thinking About the Story

*What Did You Understand?*

A. Answer the following questions in complete sentences. Write your answers in the empty spaces. Then compare your answers with those of a classmate. Your teacher may wish to put these questions on the walls of your classroom and ask you to walk around with a partner answering the questions. Then each of you could take down one question and read it out loud, so that the whole class can talk about it.

1. Give several reasons why Anthony Flores liked his job. Do you think that these are good reasons?

   _____

   _____

   _____

2. What was Anthony's dream?

   _____

3. Why did this dream make him unhappy?

_____

4. What did Anthony do to make Edna feel better?

_____

5. Why was Edna surprised?

_____

6. Why were the criminals caught?

_____

7. Why did Anthony move?

_____

B. Correct the sentences below according to the content of the story. Write your corrections in the blanks, and compare what you have written with a classmate.

1. Anthony wanted to be a police officer more than anything else.

_____

2. The mayor of Ludville didn't care about Anthony's work.

_____

3. Anthony didn't enjoy stopping crimes.

_____

4. Edna was crying because she had lost her keys.

_____

5. Anthony could not help Edna with her problems.

_____

## ✱ Working with Words

Below is a list of words from the story. Decide if each word has a positive (good) or a negative (bad) meaning. Put the words in the positive or the negative column below. Then sit with a partner and explain to each other why you placed the words in either the positive or the negative column.

crying          frightened       rob
danger          safe             criminals
drugs           smiling          wonderful
upset           tired            helpful
good            prizes
liked (+)       favorite

*Positive Words*                *Negative Words*

good                            crying
liked                           danger
safe                            frightened
smiling                         drugs
wonderful                       rob
Favorite                        upset
prizes                          tired
helpful                         criminals

## ✱ Working with Language

Anthony used to go to schools and talk with children. He doesn't have time to do it now.

We say *used to* when we talk about something that happened repeatedly (over and over again) in the past. In the lines on the following page, write down five things that you used to do but that you don't do any more. When you have finished writing, talk with a classmate about the things you used to do and tell your classmate why you no longer do these things.

1. I used to

_____.

2. I used to

_____.

3. I used to

_____.

4. I used to

_____.

5. I used to

_____.

## ❋ Asking Questions

Following are answers to questions. Working with a partner, decide what the questions are. Write your questions in the blank spaces and compare your questions with those of other students.

1. _____?

Answer: Because he came to their school and talked to them about being safe.

2. _____?

Answer: Diana was Anthony's girlfriend.

3. _____?

Answer: Because he had caught some people who were trying to sell drugs to the children.

4. _____?

Answer: A medal.

5. _____?

Answer: He wanted to be an artist.

## ✳ Rewriting the Story

Below is the story you just read, only now words are missing from it. Some of the blanks need only one word in them. Others need several words. First, fill in as many of the missing words as you can on your own. Then, working with a classmate, fill in the rest of the blanks to make the story complete. Check this story with the complete story.

# *The Artist*

ANTHONY FLORES was a very good policeman. He had
1. _____ at the Ludville Police Department for ten
years and everyone in Ludville liked him. Anthony
2. _____ his work. He liked to do everything from
directing traffic to stopping 3. _____. He often went to
schools and talked to children about how to be safe on the streets or
about the 4. _____ of using drugs. Twice, Anthony had
caught criminals who tried 5. _____ a bank in town. He
also caught three adults who were trying to sell drugs to teenagers in
the school parking lot. Because of all the good things Anthony did,
the 6. _____ of Ludville gave him a medal. Anthony
seemed to have the life that everyone 7. _____ about.

But Anthony wasn't happy. He liked to help others, but
being a policeman was not what Anthony really wanted to do. All
his life, Anthony dreamed about being an artist. He loved
8. _____. In high school, he had drawn pictures of all kinds
of people, from farmers to movie stars. He had drawn a picture of
his parents sitting by the fire and drawn a picture of his
9. _____, Diana, feeding her horse. All of Anthony's
pictures looked just like the 10. _____ he painted, and in
high school Anthony won many 11. _____ for his
wonderful artwork.

58

But now Anthony didn't have 12. _____ to draw pictures. Being a policeman took a lot of 13. _____ work. At the end of the day, Anthony was always too 14. _____ to be an artist. Because Anthony couldn't be a policeman and an artist at the same time, he was very 15. _____.

One day Mrs. Edna Lewis, the owner of the largest 16. _____ in Ludville, came running into the police station. She was 17. _____, her dress was torn, and there was a huge 18. _____ on her face. Anthony brought Edna a cup of coffee and calmly said, "Please, Edna, tell me what has happened."

Edna was so frightened and 19. _____ that she could barely talk. "Two men with guns came into the store—" She couldn't finish her sentence. She started crying again.

"Please, Edna," said Anthony. "I can't help you if you don't tell me what happened."

So, between sobs, Edna 20. _____ how the men had made everyone in the store lie down on the floor while one man pointed his gun at her. The men demanded that she give them all of the money in the cash register. Then one of them hit her across the face. He pushed her down and both men ran out of the store.

"Do you remember what the men 21. _____ like?" Anthony asked Edna.

"I—I think so," Edna said, "One had a mustache and big—"

"Wait a minute," Anthony interrupted. He went to his desk and came back with a notepad and a pencil. As Edna talked, Anthony began 22. _____. He drew every detail that Edna could remember. When Edna was finished 23. _____ the men, Anthony showed her his drawings. Edna was 24. _____.

"I can't believe it!" she said. "These pictures look exactly like those men. You are a real artist, Anthony—even better than a

25. _____!"

Anthony made copies of his pictures and posted them all over Ludville. Three days later, a woman 26. _____ the criminals and helped the police find them.

But that was only the beginning for Anthony. Suddenly everyone wanted Anthony to draw pictures to help them. There were other store owners who had been robbed, families with

27. _____ children, and even people who had lost their pets. Anthony was drawing dozens of pictures every day from the

28. _____ people gave him. His drawings were very helpful to the Ludville police. Before long, Anthony got a job in the big city as a police artist. He moved to the city and took all of his paints, pencils, and paper with him. Now Anthony draws more people and things than he ever imagined. When Anthony goes home at night, he is still tired, but he is smiling, for he is living (and drawing) his dream.

## ❋ Retelling the Story

Working with a classmate, tell each other the story in your own words. Use the following words and expressions to help you.

> direct traffic and stop crimes
> mayor
> a dream
> loved to draw
> Diana feeding her horse
> prizes
> Edna could barely talk
> money in the cash register
> better than a photographer
> recognized the criminals
> moved
> both a police officer and an artist
> smiling

## ❋ Extending the Story

A. Anthony has a special talent. He knows how to draw, and it is very important for him to be able to use and develop his talent. All of us are talented in certain ways. Are you using and developing your talents? Talk about your talents with classmates in a small group.

B. A police officer's work is not easy. In small groups talk about what makes it difficult work. Ask one person in your group to take notes and tell the whole class what you decided. Then listen and comment on what your classmates have suggested. Your teacher may want to invite a police officer to talk to your class about his/her work.

# Chance or Destiny?

## ✳ Before You Read

*Talking About the Picture*

Look at the picture. Then, with a partner, answer the questions below. When you have finished talking to your partner, tell the rest of the class what you decided. Listen to the ideas of the other students.

- Do you like to dance?
- At parties, do you dance or do you watch other people dancing?
- How have the rules of dancing changed over the years? Do you think that such changes are good? Why or why not?
- Some cultures do not allow dancing. How do you feel about such a rule?
- Which one of the two young women in the picture do you think that the man intends to ask to dance with him?

Knowing the words below will help you to understand the story. Listen and repeat as your teacher reads the words. Do you know what these words mean? Ask your teacher or your classmates to help you if you need a meaning explained. Then read the story.

| | |
|---|---|
| ice cream | to reach |
| apartment | toes |
| beach | to major |
| to divorce | chance |
| nickname | polite |
| romance | community center |
| destiny | to waste |
| petals | precious |
| fashionable | impolite |
| plump | to refuse |
| curly hair | to expect |
| to march | to bump |
| to head | |

## ✸ The Story

# *Chance or Destiny?*

MY UNCLE HENRY and my Aunt Gloria have been happily married for the past forty-five years. They seem to be very much in love. I enjoy watching them together. They finish each other's sentences when they talk. Their conversations, for example, go like this: Uncle Henry begins to say "Gloria, do we have any . . . ?" And Aunt Gloria says, "Butter pecan ice cream? Yes, I got some yesterday at the grocery store, and I also got the kind of butterscotch topping you like. I'll bring you some while you watch the news." 5

Or Aunt Gloria will say, "I'm so nervous about . . ." and 10 Uncle Henry says, "flying back to Wisconsin to see the family? Well don't worry about it. You'll see once we get there, you'll really enjoy it."

Henry and Gloria live in an apartment on the beach in Florida. I like to visit them, and I love to watch them walk hand in hand on the beach. It is wonderful to see them sitting on the sofa together; Henry always puts his arm around Gloria and she strokes the back of his neck. When they talk to each other, they call each other all kinds of cute nicknames. She calls him "Cookie" or "Honey," and he calls her "Love," or "Duck," or sometimes "Squirrel."

Not many people in my family are this happily married. As a matter of fact, my parents are divorced, and so are all my other aunts and uncles. Sometimes I wonder how and why it is Henry and Gloria have been so happy together for such a long time. I haven't met the person I want to marry yet, and I worry that I never will. If I do, I really hope to have a lifetime romance like that of Henry and Gloria.

One day, I asked Aunt Gloria to tell me the secret of her happiness. She smiled and said, "Sometimes things just go right. The first time I saw your Uncle Henry, I knew that he was the man for me—that was all there was to it—it was just destiny."

"How did it happen?" I asked. "How did you and Henry meet?"

Aunt Gloria smiled. "It was at a dance," she said. "I was sitting next to Lisa Dryer, the most beautiful girl in our class. Lisa was very tall, with long blond hair and beautiful blue eyes. Her skin was like petals of a flower; she had a smile that would make all the boys go crazy. Lisa was a banker's daughter, and her family was very rich. She was the only girl in our class who drove her own car to school—a white Buick. Of course, she wore the most fashionable clothes, which made her look even more beautiful. I knew that sitting next to Lisa would not help me look pretty. I was short and a little plump, just like I am now. My hair was brown and curly, and I was very shy. I was sure that I would spend the whole night just sitting there watching Lisa dance. But then Henry came marching across the floor. He was very handsome—but quite short, so I thought there might be a chance that he was heading for me instead of Lisa. Sure enough, he reached me just about the same time that Joe Howard, the big football player, came up and asked Lisa to dance. Before I knew it, I was dancing with my Henry. He was such a good dancer. He even made me think I was a good dancer, though I stepped on his toes several times. He danced with me the whole night, and then we talked and talked. After that we went to college together, and we both majored in history. You might say that the rest *is* history.

That night, I drove to the grocery store with Uncle Henry because Aunt Gloria had forgotten to buy butter pecan ice cream.

"Uncle Henry," I said. "Aunt Gloria told me how you two met at the dance. I really think that it's a great story. Do you think that I can find my true love like that too? Is it chance or destiny?"

"I think that it's a matter of being polite," said Uncle Henry.

"Being polite?" I said, "I don't quite understand."

"Well," said Uncle Henry. "This is how it happened. My friend Ron talked me into going to a dance with him, though I didn't want to go. You see, I was working as a dance teacher at our community center, and dancing was really work for me. I danced almost every day and certainly didn't want to waste my precious Saturday night dancing. But Ron was a good friend, and I didn't want to be impolite and refuse to go with him.

When we arrived at the dance, I looked across the room and saw the most beautiful woman I had ever seen. She had long blond hair, blue eyes the color of the sky, and a smile you could die for. I hurried across the room to ask her to dance, but the second before I got the chance, a huge football player walked up and invited her to dance. Disappointed, I looked away quickly, only to notice a girl sitting in the next chair, looking up at me like she expected me to ask her to dance. Of course, I was too polite to walk away, so I invited her to dance.

Her dancing was something awful. She kept stepping on my toes and bumping into other people. Of course, as a teacher of dancing, I was used to those kinds things, and this girl was a quick

66

learner. By the time we were dancing our third dance, she was getting pretty good at it, and we were certainly having a fun time. It turned out that she was reading the same book I was reading, and she listened to the same kind of music. As you can see, I have been dancing with her ever since. You know something—I love dancing with her more and more every day!" <sup>85</sup>

After listening to Uncle Henry and Aunt Gloria, I still don't know if I am going to find the right person for me, but I've learned that at least it pays to be polite. <sup>90</sup>

## ❋ Thinking About the Story

*What Did you Understand?*

Answer the following questions in complete sentences. Write your answers in the empty spaces. Then compare your answers with those of a classmate. Your teacher may wish to put these questions on the walls of your classroom and ask you to walk around with a partner answering the questions. Then each of you could take down one question and read it out loud, so that the whole class can talk about it.

1. In what ways do we see that Henry and Gloria love each other?

_____

2. What kind of a young woman was Aunt Gloria?

_____

3. What kind of a young woman was Lisa Dryer?

_____

4. How did Gloria feel sitting next to Lisa?

_____

5. Why did Henry ask Gloria to dance?

_____

6. Why have Gloria and Henry been lucky?

_____

7. Who is telling this story—a man or a woman? Explain why you
   think the narrator is a man or why you think the narrator is a
   woman.

_____

_____

## ✸ Working with Words

A. Henry and Gloria lived in an apartment. An apartment is a
   small part of a large house. An apartment building is made up of
   many apartments. There are many words in English that are
   made from the word *part*. Here are some of them:

>       to part from someone
>       to impart knowledge
>       to depart from a place
>       the departure lounge at the airport
>       a department
>       a partner
>       a partnership
>       a partition
>       a party

Using your dictionary, work with a partner to make sure you
understand the meanings of all these words. Use each of the
words in a sentence. Read your sentences to another pair of
students and listen to your classmates' sentences. Check with
your teacher if you are not sure your sentences are correct. Can
you and your partner find even more words made from the word
*part*? Write them in the spaces on the next page. Tell the rest of
the class about your new words and their meanings.

## My New Words from the Dictionary

_____     _____

_____     _____

_____     _____

_____     _____

_____     _____

B. In English, there are many words that mean "to move forward on your legs." Here are some of them:

| | |
|---|---|
| stroll | dance |
| promenade | hop |
| walk | saunter |
| amble | hike |
| jog | pace |
| run | march |

Using your dictionary, work with a partner to make sure you understand the meanings of all these words. Use each of the words in a sentence that shows its meaning. Read your sentences to another pair of students and listen to your classmates' sentences. Check with your teacher if you are not sure your sentences are correct. Can you and your partner find even more words that mean *to move forward on your legs?* Write them in the spaces below. Tell the rest of the class about your new words and their meanings.

### My New Words from the Dictionary

_____     _____

_____     _____

_____     _____

_____     _____

_____     _____

C. In the story, Gloria steps on Henry's toes. In groups of three, starting with parts of the face, review as many parts of the body as you can remember. Tell the class your words and listen to the words of other groups. Your teacher will make a list on the board of what everyone remembers.

## ❋ Working with Language

The narrator of the story hopes to someday meet the right person to marry, his or her true love. When we hope for something, we say *I hope to* _____. For example, *I hope to write a wonderful book* or *I hope to visit Rome.* Write down three of your hopes. Then stand up and mingle. One at a time, tell each classmate what you hope to do and listen to what your classmates hope to do. Ask your classmates questions about their hopes, and be ready to answer their questions. Continue this activity until your teacher asks you to stop.

*My Hopes*

1. _____

2. _____

3. _____

## ❋ Asking Questions

Following are answers to questions. Working with a partner, decide what the questions are. Write your questions in the blank spaces and compare your questions with those of other students.

1. _____?

Answer: Forty-five years.

2. _____?

Answer: In an apartment in Florida.

3. _____?

Answer: She knew the first time she saw him.

4. _____?

   Answer: She had skin like petals of a flower.

5. _____?

   Answer: He was a dance teacher.

## ✽ Rewriting the Story

   Below is the story you just read, only now words are missing from it. Some of the blanks need only one word in them. Others need several words. First, fill in as many of the missing words as you can on your own. Then, working with a classmate, fill in the rest of the blanks to make the story complete. Check this story with the complete story.

## *Chance or* 1. _____?

MY UNCLE HENRY and my Aunt Gloria have been happily married for the past forty-five years. They seem to be very much in 2. _____. I enjoy watching them together. They finish each other's 3. _____ when they talk. Their conversations, for example, go like this: Uncle Henry begins to say "Gloria, do we have any . . . ?" And Aunt Gloria says, "Butter pecan ice cream? Yes, I got some yesterday at the 4. _____, and I also got the kind of butterscotch topping you like. I'll bring you some while you 5. _____ the news."

   Or Aunt Gloria will say, "I'm so nervous about . . ." and Uncle Henry says, "6. _____ back to Wisconsin to see the family? Well don't worry about it. You'll see once we get there, you'll really enjoy it."

   Henry and Gloria live in an apartment on the 7. _____ in Florida. I like to visit them, and I love to watch them walk hand in 8. _____ on the beach. It is wonderful

to see them sitting on the sofa together; Henry always puts his arm
9. _____ Gloria and she strokes the back of his neck. When
they talk to each other, they call each other all kinds of cute
10. _____. She calls him "Cookie" or "Honey," and he calls
her "Love," or "Duck," or sometimes "Squirrel."

Not many people in my family are this happily
11. _____. As a matter of fact, my 12. _____ are
divorced, and so are all my other aunts and uncles. Sometimes I
wonder how and why it is Henry and Gloria have been so happy
together for such a long
13. _____. I haven't met the person I want to marry yet,
and I worry that I never will. If I do, I really hope to have a lifetime
14. _____ like that of Henry and Gloria.

One day, I asked Aunt Gloria to tell me the
15. _____ of her happiness. She smiled and said,
"Sometimes things just go right. The first time I saw your Uncle
Henry, I knew that he was the man for me—that was all there was
to it—it was just 16. _____."

"How did it happen?" I asked. "How did you and Henry
meet?"

Aunt Gloria smiled. "It was at a 17. _____," she said.
"I was sitting next to Lisa Dryer, the most 18. _____ girl in
our class. Lisa was very tall, with long blond hair and beautiful blue
eyes. Her skin was like petals of a flower; she had a smile that would
make all the boys go 19. _____. Lisa was a banker's
daughter, and her family was very rich. She was the only girl in our
class who drove her own car to school—a white Buick. Of course,
she wore the most 20. _____ clothes, which made her look
even more beautiful. I knew that sitting next to Lisa would not help
me look pretty. I was short and a little 21. _____, just like I
am now. My hair was 22. _____, and I was very shy. I was
sure that I would spend the whole night just sitting there watching
Lisa dance. But then Henry came 23. _____ across the

floor. He was very handsome—but quite short, so I thought there might be a chance that he was heading for me instead of Lisa. Sure enough, he reached me just about the same time that Joe Howard, the big football player, came up and 24. _____ Lisa to dance. Before I knew it, I was dancing with my Henry. He was such a good 25. _____. He even made me think I was a good dancer, though I stepped on his toes several times. He danced with me the whole night, and then we talked and talked. After that we went to college together, and we both 26. _____ in history. You might say that the rest *is* history.

That night, I drove to the grocery store with Uncle Henry because Aunt Gloria had forgotten to buy butter pecan ice cream.

"Uncle Henry," I said. "Aunt Gloria told me how you two met at the dance. I really think that it's a great 27. _____. Do you think that I can find my true love like that too? Is it chance or destiny?"

"I think that it's a matter of being 28. _____," said Uncle Henry.

"Being polite?" I said, "I don't quite understand."

"Well," said Uncle Henry. "This is how it 29. _____. My friend Ron talked me into going to a dance with him, though I didn't want to go. You see, I was working as a dance 30. _____ at our community center, and dancing was really work for me. I danced almost every day and certainly didn't want 31. _____ my precious Saturday night dancing. But Ron was a good friend, and I didn't want to be impolite and refuse to go with him.

When we arrived at the dance, I looked across the room and saw the most beautiful woman I had ever seen. She had long blond hair, blue eyes the color of the sky, and a smile you could die for. I hurried 32. _____ the room to ask her to dance, but the second before I got the chance, a huge football player walked up and 33. _____ her to dance. Disappointed, I looked away quickly, only to notice a girl sitting in the next chair, looking up at me like she expected me to ask her to dance. Of course, I was too polite to walk away, so I invited her to dance.

Her dancing was something awful. She kept stepping on my toes and 34. _____ into other people. Of course, as a teacher of dancing, I was used to those kinds things, and this girl was a quick learner. By the time we were dancing our third dance, she was getting pretty good at it, and we were certainly having a fun time. It turned out that she was reading the same book I was reading, and she listened to the same kind of music. As you can see, I have been 35. _____ with her ever since. You know something—I love dancing with her more and more every day!"

After listening to Uncle Henry and Aunt Gloria, I still don't know if I am going to find the right person for me, but I've learned that at least it pays to be 36. _____.

## ❋ Retelling the Story

Working with a classmate, tell each other the story in your own words. Use the following words and expressions to help you.

| | |
|---|---|
| happily married | short |
| in love | very shy |
| conversations | dancing |
| Florida | friend Ron |
| nicknames | polite |
| parents divorced | hurried to ask her to dance |
| secret of happiness | big football player |
| beautiful girl | stepped on my toes |
| banker's daughter | learned fast |
| own car | pays to be polite |
| fashionable clothes | |

## ✳ Extending the Story

A. Gloria and Henry met at a dance. Is a dance still a good place for young people to meet one another? In small groups, talk about all the different places one might go to meet people. Make a list of the places you suggest. Read your suggestions to the rest of the class and listen to and comment on the suggestions of other classmates.

B. Many people today meet each other through newspaper advertisements. Below are three such advertisements. In a small group, write an answer to one of the advertisements. Your group might want to pretend that you are answering for a good friend or a relative.

### Advertisement Number One

Tall female with dark curls. People say I'm pretty. Twenty-three years old, love reading and hiking—am looking for a boyfriend who enjoys the outdoors. No smokers.

### Advertisement Number Two

Forty-three-year-old dentist. Make good money, would be a good husband. Enjoy the movies, late breakfasts in bed on Sundays. Where is my future bride?

### Advertisement Number Three

Short (5′ 3″), 36-year-old lawyer looking for a real lady. Has to be smart, interesting, professional. Want to start a family. Must be a good conversationalist and like books. Looks are less important.

C. In small groups, give advice to this
newly married couple. Ask someone
in your group to write down the
advice. Later read out what you
have suggested to the whole class.
Listen and comment on what
other students have written.

# Story 7

# Secrets

## ❋ Before You Read

*Talking About the Picture*

Look at the picture. Then, with a partner, answer the questions below. When you have finished talking to your partner, tell the rest of the class what you decided. Listen to the ideas of the other students.

• Where are the people in this picture?
• Who are the people in the picture?
• Why do you think they look so surprised?
• What do you think the relationship is between them?

Knowing the words below will help you to understand the story. Listen and repeat as your teacher reads the words. Do you know what these words mean? Ask your teacher or your classmates to help you if you need a meaning explained. Then read the story.

| | | |
|---|---|---|
| construction worker | furniture | housekeeper |
| frame | delicious | bored |
| bricks | laundry | saleswoman |
| talented | to mend | bank account |
| staircase | cozy | manager |
| comfortable | to fire | owner |
| curtains | contact | ironing |

## ❋ The Story

## Secrets

GERALD AND KATHY seemed like a happily married couple. They loved each other very much, though they each did very different things. Gerald worked as a construction worker in the town of Dingle. He would leave the house every morning to go build houses. He built all kinds of houses—wood ones, stone ones, and brick ones. He knew how to put down a floor, build a staircase, and climb high on the frames of new houses to work on windows. He was a talented and experienced builder.

Kathy stayed at home and kept house. She made their house beautiful and comfortable. Kathy knew how to sew curtains, arrange furniture, grow plants, and cook delicious meals. Every day, Kathy did something important in the house. On Mondays, she cleaned. On Tuesdays, she did the laundry. On Wednesdays, she ironed. On Thursdays, she baked bread. On Fridays, she mended socks. Kathy enjoyed doing work that made Gerald happy when he returned in the evenings.

Every day when Gerald came home, he would sit down with Kathy and tell her about everything that had happened to him at work. Kathy always looked forward to hearing about Gerald's day. He had so many interesting things happen to him! One day Gerald told Kathy about the little boy who wanted Gerald to make him a house with a glass roof so that he could count the stars at night. Another day, a builder found a bird's nest in the frame of a house, and they decided to build around it instead of move it. Kathy was amazed that Gerald always had wonderful stories to tell.

Gerald loved talking to Kathy in the evenings. He was very proud of his wife, and he would never forget to tell her how beautiful and cozy the house was, how good the food tasted, and how glad he was that Kathy washed his shirts.

Then something terrible happened. There were no more houses to build in Dingle, and Gerald lost his job. He was fired. Poor Gerald! He had saved some money in the bank, but he was really worried about Kathy. He knew that the stories about his job were Kathy's contact with the world outside of their house, and he felt that Kathy would be very unhappy if he didn't come home with interesting things to say. So Gerald made a decision. He decided that he would not tell Kathy that he had been fired. Every morning, Gerald still left the house at the same time and returned with interesting stories to tell. Of course, none of the stories were true anymore.

But Kathy had also made a decision. She had been getting very bored at home, so she decided to go out and find a job. She knew that Gerald was proud of her for keeping the house pretty, so she didn't tell him that she was looking for a job. One day Kathy found a job as a saleswoman in the dress department of a large store. Kathy loved the work. She enjoyed meeting different people, and she had fun helping women find dresses they liked.

Every morning after Gerald left for work, Kathy quickly did her housework and then went to her job in the store. She was always home before Gerald; she still cooked wonderful food; and she still kept the house clean and cozy. Therefore, Gerald never found out about her new job. Soon Kathy opened a bank account, and every week she added more and more money to it. One day, the manager of her department moved away, and the owner of the store asked Kathy to be the new manager. Kathy was so excited; now she made even more money and had even more exciting responsibilities! <sub>55</sub>

When Gerald had been out of work for a month, he started to worry about money. He knew that finally he had to tell Kathy the truth, so he came home in the middle of the day. The day was Wednesday, and Gerald expected Kathy to be home ironing his shirts. Gerald was so surprised when he found his shirts hanging in the closet, every one of them clean and ironed—but no one at home! Gerald was very worried. Three hours later, Kathy opened the door. She was wearing a beautiful red dress that Gerald had never seen before, and her hair was combed and curled. Gerald turned white with fear. Suddenly he had some very ugly thoughts.

Gerald and Kathy sat down together on the sofa. Now it was time for both of them to tell their stories. First Gerald talked. Then Kathy talked. When they both realized what had happened, they kissed and hugged and kissed again.

The next day, Gerald put on his navy blue suit and went with Kathy to the store where she worked. The owner needed a salesperson in the tool department, and Gerald got the job. Now Gerald and Kathy meet for lunch every day. They tell each other interesting stories about their jobs, and on the weekends they work in the house together. The house is still beautiful, comfortable, and clean—it's a good place to come home to!

## ❋ Thinking About the Story

*What Did You Understand?*

Answer the following questions in complete sentences. Write your answers in the empty spaces. Then compare your answers with those of a classmate. Your teacher may wish to put these questions on the walls of your classroom and ask you to walk around with a partner answering the questions. Then each of you could take down one question and read it out loud, so that the whole class can talk about it.

1. What was good and what was bad about the way Gerald and Kathy used to live?

_____

2. Why did Gerald feel that he had to lie to Kathy?

_____

3. Why did Kathy feel that she had to keep her job a secret from Gerald?

_____

4. What did Gerald think when he saw Kathy at the door?

_____

5. How did the lives of Gerald and Kathy change?

_____

## ❋ Working with Words

The table on the next page has many forms of the same word. Study the table and then with a partner quiz each other to see if you know all the forms. Then look at the second table, where some of the words have been left out. First, fill in all the blanks you can remember by yourself, then check with a partner to see if you got them right. Finally, look back at the first table to check your answers. When you think that you know all the forms of the words, choose one word and write sentences using the different forms. Read your sentences to the class.

Example Sentences:
We meet every day.
Today we really had a good meeting.

## The Word Family Table

| Verb | Noun | Adjective | Adverb |
|------|------|-----------|--------|
| to construct | a construction | constructive | constructively |
| to work | work, a worker | working | X |
| to build | building, a builder | X | X |
| to frame | a frame | X | X |
| X | happiness | happy | happily |
| to marry | marriage | married | X |
| to experience | an experience | experienced | X |
| to comfort | comfort | comfortable | comfortably |
| to beautify | beauty | beautiful | beautifully |
| to meet | meeting | X | X |
| X | truth | true, truthful | truthfully |
| to own | ownership, owner | X | X |
| to sell | a sale, a salesperson, a salesman, a salesclerk, a saleswoman | sold | X |
| to interest | an interest | interesting, interested | interestingly |

## The Fill-in-the-Word Family Table

| Verb | Noun | Adjective | Adverb |
|---|---|---|---|
| to construct | | | |
| to work | | | |
| to build | | | |
| to frame | | | |
| | happiness | | |
| to marry | | | |
| to experience | | | |
| | comfort | | |
| | beauty | | |
| to meet | | | |
| | truth | | |
| to own | | | |
| to sell | | | |
| to interest | | | |

## ✳ Working with Language

You may have noticed that the verb *to interest* made two adjectives—*interested* and *interesting*. There are many verbs that make two adjectives. Below are some examples:

> *To amuse* makes *amused* and *amusing*.
> *To amaze* makes *amazed* and *amazing*.
> *To fascinate* makes *fascinated* and *fascinating*.
> *To surprise* makes *surprised* and *surprising*.
> *To bore* makes *bored* and *boring*.
> *To disturb* makes *disturbed* and *disturbing*.

We use the *-ing* form to describe someone or something. We use the *-ed* form to tell how we feel about something.

Example: It was a very *interesting* lesson. (This sentence describes the lesson.) All the students were *interested* in what the teacher had to say. (This sentence tells us how the students felt about the lesson.)

In the sentences below, write the correct form of each adjective. Compare your answers with those of a partner. Then ask other students in your class to write the correct answers on the board so that everyone can check his/her answers.

1. (to surprise) I was very _____ when I heard the _____ news on the radio.

2. (to amaze) He is an _____ artist. People look at his pictures with _____ expressions on their faces. They feel so _____ by his work.

3. (to bore) It was a very _____ lesson. All the students looked so _____. The teacher gave the same _____ talk he had given his other class.

4. (to disturb) He told me a very _____ story. I felt _____ the whole day when I thought about it.

## ✳ Asking Questions

Following are answers to questions. Working with a partner, decide what the questions are. Write your questions in the blank spaces and compare your questions with those of other students.

1. _____?

    Answer: He was a construction worker.

2. _____?

    Answer: Kathy was a good cook.

3. _____?

    Answer: Gerald would tell Kathy stories about what happened at work.

4. _____?

    Answer: Gerald lost his job.

5. _____?

    Answer: He decided to tell Kathy the truth.

# ✳ Rewriting the Story

Below is the story you just read, only now words are missing from it. Some of the blanks need only one word in them. Others need several words. First, fill in as many of the missing words as you can on your own. Then, working with a classmate, fill in the rest of the blanks to make the story complete. Check this story with the complete story.

## Secrets

GERALD AND KATHY seemed like a happily 1. _____ couple. They loved each other very much, though they each did very 2. _____ things. Gerald worked as a 3. _____ worker in the town of Dingle. He would leave the house every morning to go 4. _____ houses. He built all kinds of houses—wood ones, stone ones, and brick ones. He knew how to put down a floor, build a staircase, and climb high on the frames of new houses to work on windows. He was a talented and experienced 5. _____.

Kathy stayed at home and kept house. She made their house beautiful and comfortable. Kathy knew how to sew 6. _____, arrange furniture, grow plants, and cook 7. _____ meals. Every day, Kathy did something important in the house. On Mondays, she 8. _____. On Tuesdays, she did the 9. _____. On Wednesdays, she ironed. On Thursdays, she 10. _____ bread. On Fridays, she 11. _____ socks. Kathy enjoyed doing work that made Gerald happy when he returned in the evenings.

Every day when Gerald came home, he would sit down with Kathy and tell her about everything that 12. _____ to him at work. Kathy always looked forward to hearing about Gerald's day. He had so many 13. _____ things happen to him! One day Gerald told Kathy about the little boy who wanted Gerald to make him a house with a glass roof so that he could count the stars at night. Another day, a builder found a bird's nest in the frame of a house, and they decided to build around it instead of move it. Kathy was 14. _____ that Gerald always had wonderful stories to tell.

Gerald loved talking to Kathy in the evenings. He was very 15. _____ of his wife, and he would never forget to tell her how beautiful and cozy the house was, how good the food tasted, and how glad he was that Kathy washed his shirts.

Then something 16. _____ happened. There were no more houses to build in Dingle, and Gerald lost his job. He was 17. _____. Poor Gerald! He had 18. _____ some money in the bank, but he was really worried about Kathy. He knew that the stories about his job were Kathy's contact with the world 19. _____ of their house, and he felt that Kathy would be very unhappy if he didn't come home with interesting things to say. So Gerald made a 20. _____. He decided that he would not tell Kathy that he had been fired. Every morning, Gerald still 21. _____ the house at the same time and returned with interesting stories to tell. Of course, none of the stories were 22. _____ anymore.

But Kathy had also made a decision. She had been getting very 23. _____ at home, so she decided to go out and find a job. She knew that Gerald was proud of her for keeping the house pretty, so she didn't tell him that she was looking for a job. One day Kathy found a job as a 24. _____ in the dress department of a large store. Kathy loved the work. She enjoyed meeting different people, and she had fun helping women 25. _____ dresses they liked.

Every morning after Gerald left for work, Kathy 26. _____did her housework and then went to her job in the store. She was always home before Gerald; she still cooked wonderful food; and she still kept the house clean and

27. _____. Therefore, Gerald never found out about her new job. Soon Kathy opened a 28. _____, and every week she added more and more money to it. One day, the manager of her department moved away, and the owner of the store asked Kathy to be the new 29. _____. Kathy was so excited; now she made even more money and had even more exciting responsibilities!

When Gerald had been out of work for a month, he started to worry about money. He knew that finally he had to tell Kathy 30. _____, so he came home in the middle of the day. The day was Wednesday, and Gerald expected Kathy to be home ironing his shirts. Gerald was so surprised when he found his shirts hanging in the closet, every one of them clean and 31. _____—but no one at home! Gerald was very worried. Three hours later, Kathy opened the door. She 32. _____ a beautiful red dress that Gerald had never seen before, and her hair was combed and curled. Gerald turned white with fear. Suddenly he had some very ugly thoughts.

Gerald and Kathy sat down together on the sofa. Now it was time for both of them to tell their stories. First Gerald talked. Then Kathy talked. When they both realized what had happened, they kissed and hugged and kissed again.

The next day, Gerald put on his navy blue suit and went with Kathy to the store where she worked. The owner needed a salesperson in the tool department, and Gerald got the job. Now Gerald and Kathy 33. _____ for lunch every day. They tell each other interesting stories about their jobs, and on the 34. _____ they work in the house together. The house is still beautiful, comfortable, and clean—it's a good place to 35. _____ to!

## ❋ Retelling the Story

Working with a classmate, tell each other the story in your own words. Use the following words and expressions to help you.

| | |
|---|---|
| happily married | loved her job |
| building houses | came home |
| proud | very surprised |
| kept house | ugly thoughts |
| fired | hugged and kissed |
| made a decision | tool department |
| bored | meet for lunch |
| saleswoman | good place |

## ❋ Extending the Story

A. In small groups, talk about the questions below. Ask one person in your group to take notes. Later tell the whole class about your conclusions, and listen to what the other groups have to say.

1. At the beginning of the story, do you believe that Kathy and Gerald really had a happy marriage? Why or why not?

2. How does the marriage change? Do you think that it is a change for the better? Why or why not?

B. Following are sentences that describe marriage. Listen and repeat as your teacher reads the sentences to you. In the space after each sentence write the word *agree* if you agree with the sentence. Write *disagree* if you disagree and write *not sure* if you are not sure about the sentence. Then get up and mingle. Talk with each classmate about one sentence only. Tell each classmate how you have marked your sentence, and explain why you have marked it that way. Then listen to what each of your classmates has to say.

1. In a good marriage, the husband and wife share all the money.

   _____

2. In a good marriage, the wife and husband have no secrets from each other.

   _____

3. In a good marriage, the husband and wife do the housework together.

   _____

4. In a good marriage, the wife takes care of the children.

   _____

5. In a good marriage, the husband makes all the money.

   _____

6. In a good marriage, the husband and wife like doing the same things.

   _____

7. In a good marriage, the husband and wife have all the same friends.

   _____

8. In a good marriage, the husband is taller than the wife.

   _____

9. In a good marriage, the husband is older than the wife.

   _____

10. In a good marriage, the husband is smarter than the wife.

    _____

C. In the story, we learned that when Kathy and Gerald discovered each other's secrets, they talked a lot to explain what had happened, but we don't know what they said. In small groups,

- talk about what they might have said.
- write down what they said.
- ask your teacher to help you correct what you have written.
- practice reading what you have written.
- ask two students from your group to read the conversation to the whole class.
- listen to the conversations of other students.

D. In a family, should there be secrets like the secrets that Gerald and Kathy had? Why or why not?

Story 8

# Plenty of Room

## ✳ Before You Read

*Talking About the Picture*

Look at the picture. Then, with a partner, answer the questions below. When you have finished talking to your partner, tell the rest of the class what you decided. Listen to the ideas of the other students.

- Who are the people in the picture?
- What animals are in the picture?
- Why do you think these people are living with animals?
- Do you think these people have a lot of money?
- Where do you think they live?

Knowing the words below will help you to understand the story. Listen and repeat as your teacher reads the words. Do you know what these words mean? Ask your teacher or your classmates to help you if you need a meaning explained. Then read the story.

| | | |
|---|---|---|
| village | to trust | pig |
| upset | serious | chickens |
| to complain | strange | to shout |
| cooking pots | crowded | headache |
| advice | cow | |

## ❋ The Story

# *Plenty of Room*

I N A LITTLE VILLAGE a long time ago a farmer by the name of Ivan was very upset because his house was too small. The farmer had a wife and five children, and there never seemed to be enough space for all of them. The farmer's wife complained that she didn't have a place for her cooking pots, the children were always fighting with one another for a place to play, and poor Ivan had no place to sit and rest after he finished his long, hard day of work. Finally, Ivan decided that he needed some advice. He asked his friends, and they all suggested that he should go and see old Gregor. 5 10

Old Gregor was the wise old man of the village. Everyone in the village trusted Gregor because he always gave such good advice.

"Dear Gregor," said Ivan, "you know how to do things right. Please help me. My house is too small, and I don't have enough money to build a larger one. What should I do?" 15

"This is indeed a serious problem," Gregor said, "but I think I can help you."

"Oh, dear Gregor," said the poor farmer, "if only you could."

"Do you have a pig?" Gregor asked.

"Yes, of course," Ivan answered.

"Then," said Gregor, "bring the pig into your house to live with you."

Ivan thought that this advice was very strange, but he had much respect for Gregor, so when he came home he told his wife that from now on the pig would live in the house with them.

As you probably guessed, things did not get any better—they got worse. The house was terribly crowded. Ivan's wife was always shouting, the children were always fighting, and poor Ivan got a very bad headache. So, he returned to Gregor.

"Dear Gregor," he said, "this is a terrible thing, and I don't like to complain to you, but life in my house is very bad. It was no help at all to bring in the pig. The house seems smaller and more crowded than it ever was. Please, please tell me what to do."

"This is indeed a very serious problem," Gregor said, "but I think that I can help you. Do you have a cow?"

"Yes, of course," Ivan answered.

"Then," said Gregor, "bring the cow into the house to live with you."

Now this was really strange advice, but Ivan really respected old Gregor, so he went home and told his wife that from now on the cow would have to live in the house with them. As you can probably guess, things did not get better. It just got more and more crowded. Ivan's wife was angry, the children were fighting not just with one another but also with the pig and the cow, the house was smelly and dirty, and everyone hated everyone else. After a week's time, Ivan returned to old Gregor.

"Dear Gregor," he said, "this time you really must help me. Life in our house is impossible. It is more crowded than ever. My wife is always shouting, the children are always fighting, and I have such a terrible headache. Please help us, dear Gregor."

"This is indeed a serious problem," said old Gregor, "but I think that I can help you. Do you have any chickens?"

"Yes, of course," said Ivan.

"Then," said old Gregor, "bring the chickens into your house to live with you." 55

This was very strange advice, but, as you know, Ivan respected the advice of old Gregor, so he went home and told his wife that from now on all ten of their chickens would have to live in the house with them.

You can imagine how difficult life became in the little cottage. Wherever the cow wasn't waving its tail, the pig was rolling around, or one of the children was sitting on a newly laid egg— squish, squash—what a mess! 60

Ivan hurried to old Gregor, "Help! Help!" he shouted, "Help! Help!" 65

"Yes, my dear friend," said old Gregor calmly. "Go home now, and take all those animals out of the house."

Ivan did as he was told, and the whole family cleaned the house from top to bottom. What a lovely house! How nice and clean everything looked! And it was so quiet! There was plenty of space for everyone. The family loved their new home. 70

That day, when Ivan met old Gregor in front of the village church, Ivan smiled and shook Gregor's hand. "Your advice was wonderful as always," he said. "You have given us a new house with plenty of room." 75

## ✼ Thinking About the Story

### *What Did You Understand?*

Answer the following questions in complete sentences. Write your answers in the empty spaces. Then compare your answers with those of a classmate. Your teacher may wish to put these questions on the walls of your classroom and ask you to walk around with a partner answering the questions. Then each of you could take down one question and read it out loud, so that the whole class can talk about it.

1. Why did Ivan need advice?

_____

2. Why did Ivan go to Gregor?

_____

3. What kind of woman is Ivan's wife?

_____

4. Why was Gregor's advice strange?

_____

5. What happened each time Ivan followed Gregor's advice?

_____

6. Why did the family suddenly have plenty of room?

_____

## ❋ Working with Words

In each group of words below, there is one word that does not belong. Working with a partner, decide which word is the one that does not belong and explain why it doesn't fit with the other words. You and your partner might want to check your answers with those of another pair.

|  |  |  |  |
|---|---|---|---|
| 1. village | town | ocean | city |
| 2. headache | advice | earache | broken arm |
| 3. crowded | empty | pretty | full |
| 4. complained | shouted | jumped | answered |
| 5. advice | bread | cheese | apples |
| 6. upset | angry | ashamed | happy |
| 7. wise | stupid | clever | intelligent |
| 8. serious | smiling | happy | laughing |
| 9. strange | ordinary | foreign | odd |
| 10. cooking pots | frying pans | pitchers | chairs |

## ❋ Working with Language

Decide which phrase has the same meaning as the phrase in the story. Choose the answer you think is the best one and later compare your answers with a partner.

1. "There never seemed to be enough space for all of them." (lines 3-4)
   a. It was always too crowded.
   b. There was enough space.
   c. There seemed to be enough space.
   d. It was never crowded.

2. "This is indeed a serious problem." (line 16)
   a. The problem is not very serious.
   b. The problem is easy to fix.
   c. The problem is not easy to understand.
   d. The problem is very serious.

3. "Wherever the cow wasn't waving its tail, the pig was rolling around." (line 61)
   a. The pig and the cow played together.
   b. There was not much space because the animals took up all the room.
   c. The pig and the cow both waved their tails.
   d. The pig and the cow rolled around together.

4. "He needed some advice." (lines 8-9)
   a. He needed to talk to someone.
   b. He needed someone to listen to him.
   c. He needed someone to tell him what to do.
   d. He needed someone to think for him.

5. "The children were always fighting with one another for a place to play." (lines 5-6)
   a. The children were fighting because they didn't know how to play.
   b. The children were fighting because they all wanted the same place.
   c. The children were fighting because they wanted to play with the same animal.
   d. The children were fighting because they didn't have enough space to play.

6. "Ivan respected the advice of old Gregor, so he went home and told his wife that from now on all ten of their chickens would have to live in the house with them." (lines 56-59)
   a. Ivan followed Gregor's advice.
   b. Ivan did not follow Gregor's advice.
   c. Ivan told his wife that the chickens had to go out.
   d. Gregor told Ivan to put the chickens out.

7. "As you probably guessed, things did not get any better." (line 26)
   a. Things got better.
   b. Things got worse.
   c. Things stayed the same.
   d. You guessed right.

## ✳ Asking Questions

Following are answers to questions. Working with a partner, decide what the questions are. Write your questions in the blank spaces and compare your questions with those of other students.

1. _____?

    Answer: Because his house was so small.

2. _____?

    Answer: Five.

3. _____?

    Answer: He decided to talk to Gregor.

4. _____?

    Answer: Old Gregor was the wise old man of the village.

5. _____?

    Answer: Finally, the family was happy because they had enough
    space.

## ✳ Rewriting the Story

Below is the story you just read, only now words are missing from it. Some of the blanks need only one word in them. Others need several words. First, fill in as many of the missing words as you can on your own. Then, working with a classmate, fill in the rest of the blanks to make the story complete. Check this story with the complete story.

1. _____ *of Room*

IN A LITTLE 2. _____ a long time ago a farmer by the name of Ivan was very upset because his house was 3. _____. The farmer had a wife and five 4. _____, and there never seemed to be 5. _____ space for all of them. The farmer's wife 6. _____ that she didn't have a place for her cooking pots, the children were always

7. _____ with one another for a place to play, and poor Ivan had no place to sit and rest after he 8. _____ his long, hard day of work. Finally, Ivan decided that he needed some advice. He asked his friends, and they all 9. _____ that he should go and see old Gregor.

Old Gregor was the 10. _____ old man of the village. Everyone in the village 11. _____ Gregor because he always gave such good advice.

"Dear Gregor," said Ivan, "you know how to do things right. Please help me. My house is small, and I don't have enough money to build a larger one. What should I do?"

"This is indeed a 12. _____ problem," Gregor said, "but I think I can help you."

"Oh, dear Gregor," said the poor farmer, "if only you could."

"Do you have a 13. _____?" Gregor asked.

"Yes, of course," Ivan answered.

"Then," said Gregor, "bring the pig into 14. _____ to live with you."

Ivan thought that this advice was very 15. _____, but he had much 16. _____ for Gregor, so when he came home, he told his wife that from now on the pig would live in the house with them.

As you probably 17. _____, things did not get any better—they got 18. _____ The house was 19. _____ crowded. Ivan's wife was always 20. _____, the children were always 21. _____, and poor Ivan got a very bad headache. So, he 22. _____ to Gregor.

"Dear Gregor," he said, "this is a terrible thing, and I don't like to complain to you, but life in my house is very bad. It was no help at all to bring in the pig. The house seems smaller and more crowded than it ever was. Please, please 23. _____ what to do."

"This is 24. _____ a very serious problem," Gregor said, "but I think that I can help you. Do you have a cow?"

"Yes, of course," Ivan answered.

"Then," said Gregor, 25. _____ the cow into the house to live with you."

Now this was really strange advice, but Ivan really respected old Gregor, so he went 26. _____ and told his wife that from now on the cow would have to live in the 27. _____ with them. As you can 28. _____ guess, things did not get better. It just got more and more crowded. Ivan's wife was 29. _____, the children were fighting not just with one another but also with the 30. _____ and the 31. _____ the house was 32. _____ and dirty, and everyone hated everyone else. Ater a week's time, Ivan returned to 33. _____ Gregor.

"Dear Gregor," he said, "this time you really must help me. Life in our house is 34. _____. It is more crowded than ever. My wife is always shouting, the children are always fighting, and I have such a terrible 35. _____ Please help us, dear Gregor."

"This is indeed a serious problem," said old Gregor, "but I think that I can 36. _____you. Do you have any 37. _____?"

"Yes, 38. _____," said Ivan

"Then," said old Gregor, "bring the chickens into your house to live with you."

This was very strange advice, but, as you know, Ivan respected the 39. _____ of old Gregor, so he went home and told his wife that from now on all ten of their chickens would have 40. _____ the house with them.

You can imagine how 41. _____ life became in the little cottage. Wherever the cow wasn't waving its 42. _____, the pig was rolling around, or one of the children was sitting on a newly laid egg—squish, squash—what a 43. _____!

Ivan hurried to old Gregor. "Help! Help!" he shouted, "Help! Help!"

"Yes, my dear friend," said old Gregor 44. _____. "Go home now, and take all those animals out of the house."

Ivan did as he was told, and the whole family 45. _____ the house from top to bottom. What a lovely house! How nice and clean everything looked! And it was so quiet! There was plenty of space for everyone. The family loved their new home.

That day, when Ivan met old Gregor in front of the village 46. _____, Ivan smiled and shook Gregor's hand. "Your advice was 47. _____ as always," he said. "You have given us a new house with 48. _____ of room."

## ❋ Retelling the Story

Working with a classmate, tell each other the story in your own words. Use the following words and expressions to help you.

| | |
|---|---|
| too small | cow |
| five children | more crowded |
| always fighting | chickens |
| wise old man | lovely house |
| serious problem | new home |
| pig | plenty of room |
| terribly crowded | |

## ✳ Expanding the Story

A. Below are many possible meanings for the story you have read.
   Which one of them do you think is the most important one?
   Choose one and put a circle around it, or write your idea of
   what the story means in the blank next to *Other*. Then stand up
   and mingle. Talk to your classmates one at a time. Tell each
   classmate which meaning you chose (or read your own
   meaning), and explain why you think that this is the best way to
   understand the story. Listen to what your classmates have to say.
   Continue this activity until the teacher stops you.

   Be satisfied with what you have.

   It's better to be rich than to be poor.

   Always try to get the advice of a wise person.

   Build a house that is not too crowded.

   Everything in life is relative.

   Your happiness depends on how you feel about things.

   The same place might feel very different at different times.

   Other: _____.

B. Does this story remind you of a time in your life or the life of
   someone you know when advice was needed? Share your
   thoughts with the rest of the class.

Story 9

# The Custodian

## ❋ Before You Read

*Talking About the Picture*

Look at the picture. Then, with a partner, answer the questions below. When you have finished talking to your partner, tell the rest of the class what you decided. Listen to the ideas of the other students.

- Why do you think that the man in the picture looks worried?
- Do you think that he wants to go into the church?
  Why or why not?
- What do you think the man does?

Listen and repeat when your teacher reads the words and phrases below. Do you know what these words mean? Ask your teacher or fellow students to help you if you need the meaning explained. Then read the story.

| | | |
|---|---|---|
| to polish | illiterate | opportunity |
| to shine | disgrace | to discover |
| altar | to invite | decision |
| a taste of heaven | back and forth | owner |
| to elect | neighborhood | successful |
| plans | to imagine | loan |
| | market | sign |

## ✸ The Story

# The Custodian

EDWARD SMITH was the custodian in a large downtown church. His job was to clean and look after the church. Edward loved his work. He loved polishing the large colorful windows until they shone. He loved cleaning the altar, and he loved putting flowers all around to make the church smell like a garden. When people came to church on Sunday, Edward wanted them to have a "taste of heaven" just by looking at the shiny windows, clean altar, and fresh flowers. Edward had been working in this church for fifteen years, and he was so happy that he was sure that he would work there for the rest of his life.

Then one day, the people elected a new person to run the church. The new man, Mr. Summers, invited Edward to his office and gave him a letter. "Read this letter carefully, Edward," he said. "In the letter, I have written all my plans for the church."

"I am sorry, sir," Edward said, "but I cannot read your letter."

"What do you mean?" Mr. Summers asked.

"Just what I said, sir. I cannot read the letter."

"Do you mean," said Mr. Summers, "that you don't want to read my letter?"

"No," Edward said, "I mean that I can't read!"

"What!" shouted Mr. Summers. "Do you mean that you are illiterate?"

"I mean that I can't read," said Edward very unhappily. "I never learned how."

"What a disgrace!" Mr. Summers shouted. "We can't possibly have an illiterate custodian in this church."

And that is how Edward lost his wonderful job. You can imagine how sad Edward was. He walked up and down the long street in front of the church feeling very sorry for himself. He felt as if his life had come to an end. What was he going to do without his wonderful church? How would he make a living? What opportunities are there for a person who cannot read?

After he had walked back and forth for many hours, he suddenly felt very hungry. He decided to try to find something to eat, so he walked all over the neighborhood looking for a restaurant or a food market. As Edward looked and looked, he discovered something he had not noticed before. There were no restaurants and no food markets in the whole neighborhood. "This is interesting," Edward thought. "There are probably a lot of people in this neighborhood who would like to buy food here." Right then and there Edward made an important decision. He decided that he was going to be the man who sold food in this neighborhood.

The very next day, Edward set up a little fruit stand. He sold apples, oranges, and strawberries. The following week, he sold cakes and coffee, too. Before long, Edward had enough money to open a small restaurant. Edward worked hard. He discovered that he loved to manage the restaurant and provide food for the neighborhood. In a year's time, Edward was the proud owner of three restaurants, and he was thinking about opening a restaurant in another part of town. He was by now such a successful businessman that he had no trouble at all getting a loan from the biggest bank in town. On the day when Edward went to the bank to get his loan, the bank manager gave him a letter and said, "Before you sign the loan, I would like for you to read this letter."

"Sorry," said Edward. "I can't read the letter. I never learned to read. I am illiterate." 55

The bank manager was completely <u>amazed.</u> "You have been such a successful businessman, Mr. Smith, and you can't read? Just imagine what you could have done if you had only learned how to read!" 60

"Oh, I know exactly what I would have done if I had learned to read," Edward said. "I would have been a custodian at the church downtown!"

## ❋ Thinking About the Story

*What Did You Understand?*

A. Answer the following questions in complete sentences. Write your answers in the empty spaces. Then compare your answers with those of a classmate. Your teacher may wish to put these questions on the walls of your classroom and ask you to walk around with a partner answering the questions. Then each of you could take down one question and read it out loud, so that the whole class can talk about it.

1. Why did Edward love his work?

   He loved cleaning so that the church looked beautiful.

2. Why did Edward lose his job?

   He was illiterate.

3. How did Edward feel after he had lost his job?

   He was sad and upset.

4. What did Edward suddenly discover?

   There were no markets and no restaurants.

108

5. What was the result of his discovery?

_He started selling food._

6. Why was the bank manager so surprised?

_He was surprised that Edward_
_was illiterate_

7. Do you think that Edward is happier now?

_He is happy because he is_
_working._

8. What can we learn from Edward's story?

_Don't give up - you can find a new_
_passion - new reason for living_

B. Correct the sentences below according to the content of the story. Write your corrections in the blanks and compare what you have written with a classmate. _True!_

       _NOT_
1. Edward was lazy.

_____

     _did_
2. Edward didn't enjoy working in the church. — _F_

_____

      _Not_
3. Mr. Summers was proud of Edward.

_____

4. Edward had a family.

_don't know_

5. Edward was successful in life.

_yes._

## ✳ Working with Words

Match each word in Column A with its opposite in Column B.

| Column A | Column B |
|----------|----------|
| downtown | small |
| literate | whisper |
| success | borrow |
| shout | suburbs |
| lend | illiterate |
| loved | hated |
| large | failure |

## ✳ Working with Language

Edward was a custodian. A custodian is someone who cleans and looks after a building. Later, Edward decided that he would be the man who sold food in the neighborhood.

Using the pattern of the above example, complete the sentences below in any way you wish. Then compare your sentences with those of a classmate. *relative phrase*

1. A doctor is someone who
   *treats patients for their medical.*
   *problems.*

2. A salesperson is someone who

   _____.

3. A lawyer is someone who

   _____.

4. A carpenter is someone who

   _____.

5. A teacher is someone who

   _____.

## ❋ Asking Questions

Following are answers to questions. Working with a partner, decide what the questions are. Write your questions in the blank spaces and compare your questions with those of other students.

1. _____?

    Answer: Edward wanted them to have a taste of heaven.

2. _____?

    Answer: Edward had been working in the church for fifteen years.

3. _____?

    Answer: "I mean that I can't read."

4. _____?

    Answer: He felt as if his life had come to an end.

5. _____?

    Answer: Opening a restaurant in another part of town.

## ❋ Rewriting the Story

Below is the story you just read, only now words are missing from it. Some of the blanks need only one word in them. Others need several words. First, fill in as many of the missing words as you can on your own. Then, working with a classmate, fill in the rest of the blanks to make the story complete. Check this story with the complete story.

# The Custodian

EDWARD SMITH was the custodian in a large downtown church. His job was to clean and 1._____ the church. Edward loved his work. He loved polishing the large colorful windows until they shone. He loved cleaning the 2._____, and he loved 3._____ flowers all around to make the church smell like a garden. When people came to church on Sunday, Edward wanted them to have a "taste of

4. _____" just by looking at the shiny windows, clean altar, and fresh flowers. Edward had been working in this church for fifteen years, and he was so happy that he was sure he would work there for the 5. _____ of his life.

Then one day, the people 6. _____ a new person to run the church. The new man, Mr. Summers, 7. _____ Edward to his office and gave him a letter. "Read this letter carefully, Edward," he said. "In the letter, I have written all my 8. _____ for the church."

"I am sorry, sir," Edward said, "but I cannot read your letter."

"What do you mean?" Mr. Summers asked.

"Just what I said, sir. I 9. _____ the letter."

"Do you mean," said Mr. Summers, "that you 10. _____ to read my letter?"

"No," Edward said. "I mean that I 11. _____ read!"

"What!" shouted Mr. Summers. "Do you mean that you are 12. _____?"

"I mean that I can't read," said Edward very unhappily. "I never learned how."

"What a disgrace!" Mr. Summers 13. _____. "We can't possibly have an illiterate custodian in this church."

And that is how Edward lost his wonderful job. You can imagine how sad Edward was. He walked up and down the long street in front of the church feeling very 14. _____ for himself. He felt as if his life had come to an end. What was he going to do without his 15. _____ church? How would he make a living? What opportunities are there for a person who cannot read?

After he had walked 16. _____ for many hours, he suddenly felt very 17. _____. He decided to try to find something to eat, so he walked all over the neighborhood looking for a restaurant or a food market. As Edward looked and looked, he discovered something he had not noticed before. There were no restaurants and no 18. _____ in the whole neighborhood. "This is interesting," Edward thought. "There are probably a lot of people in this neighborhood who would like to buy food here." Right then and there Edward made an important 19. _____. He decided that he was going to be the man who sold food in this neighborhood.

The very next day, Edward set up a little fruit stand. He sold apples, oranges, and strawberries. The following week, he sold cakes and 20. _____, too. Before long, Edward had enough money to open a small restaurant. Edward worked hard. He discovered that he loved to manage the restaurant and provide food for the neighborhood. In a year's time, Edward was the proud 21. _____ of three restaurants, and he 22. _____ about opening a restaurant in another part of town. He was by now such a 23. _____ businessman that he had no trouble at all getting a 24. _____ from the biggest bank in town. On the day when Edward went to the bank to get his loan, the bank manager gave him a letter and said, "Before you sign the loan, I would like for you to read this letter."

"Sorry," said Edward. "I can't read the letter. I never learned to read. I am illiterate."

The bank manager was completely 25. _____. "You have been such a successful 26. _____, Mr. Smith, and you can't read? Just imagine what you could have done if you had only 27. _____ how to read!"

"Oh, I know exactly what I would have done if I had learned to read," Edward said. "I would have been a 28. _____ at the 29. _____ downtown!"

# �֎ Retelling the Story

Working with a classmate, tell each other the story in your own words. Use the following words and expressions to help you.

> a large downtown church
> a taste of heaven
> read this letter
> disgrace
> a grand opportunity
> restaurant
> important decision
> sell food in the neighborhood
> fruit stand
> proud owner
> bank manager
> custodian

# ✷ Extending the Story

A. What Edward thought was the worst thing in his life turned into the best thing that could have happened to him. Do such things happen in real life? Does Edward's story remind you of something that happened to you or to someone you know? Talk about your answers with classmates in a small group.

B. Talk about the questions below in small groups. Ask one person in your group to take notes, and later tell the rest of the class what you have been talking about.

1. Have you ever visited a country where you couldn't read the alphabet? How did you feel?
2. Is anything being done to help people who can't read in your country?
3. What are some problems that illiterate people have to face? Your teacher might want to invite a speaker who works in adult literacy in the community where you are now studying. Prepare some questions to ask that person.

# The Dog Who Spoke Spanish

## ✻ Before You Read

*Talking About the Picture*

Look at the picture. Then, with a partner, answer the questions below. When you have finished talking to your partner, tell the rest of the class what you decided. Listen to the ideas of the other students.

- Are the man and the dog in the picture good friends?
- Why do you think that the dog is talking to this man?
- Have you owned any animals in your life?
- Why are animals important for people?
- How much of human language do you think that animals understand?

Knowing the words below will help you to understand the story. Listen and repeat as your teacher reads the words. Do you know what these words mean? Ask your teacher or your classmates to help you if you need a meaning explained. Then read the story.

| | | |
|---|---|---|
| criminals | expensive | impossible |
| to smell | to refuse | deaf |
| healthy | dangerous | commands |
| drugs | drug smugglers | stubborn |
| to hide | patience | expert |
| coat (a dog's coat) | to train | a puppy |

## ❊ The Story

# The Dog Who Spoke Spanish

JACK RUBIN was a policeman who trained dogs. He trained big, smart dogs to help the Bridgeport Police Department find criminals. Jack's dogs knew the smell of criminals. They also knew the smell of drugs. When the dogs smelled a criminal's clothes, drugs, or something else that belonged to the criminal, they would follow the smell and lead policemen to where the criminal was hiding. Because of Jack's dogs, the police have caught many dangerous drug smugglers.

It takes a lot of time and patience for Jack to train his dogs. Sometimes it is difficult for Jack to find the right kind of dog to train. One day, Frank Johnson, the town's mayor, brought a beautiful young dog to the police department. "I thought this dog might make a good police dog," Frank told Jack. "He seems very smart."

Jack liked the dog, and he liked what he saw. The dog was big and healthy. Its coat was shiny, its eyes were bright, and it noticed everything. "He certainly looks just like the kind of dog that I enjoy training. Where did you find him?" Jack asked.

"He has been wandering around my neighborhood for the past week, and I haven't been able to find his owner," said Frank. "I've been feeding him and thought you could use him."

The kind of dog Jack needed was usually very expensive, so Jack was happy to get this dog for free. Jack named the dog "Luster" since his coat was so shiny. Jack took Luster home and began training him.

After a few days, Jack realized that something was wrong with Luster. Though Luster was a nice dog and seemed to like Jack a lot, it was impossible to train him! No matter how hard Jack tried, Luster would not listen to his commands. Poor Jack! How could he ever train a dog that didn't listen? Jack just couldn't figure out what was wrong. He knew the dog wasn't deaf, so he kept trying to train him. But the more Jack worked with Luster, the more stubborn Luster became. Most of the time, Luster just sat in front of Jack, wagging his tail and looking happy. Jack decided to give up. Luster would never be a police dog.

A week later, Jack had to leave town for a meeting. He asked Esperanza Lamas, his neighbor, to take care of Luster. Esperanza loved dogs, so she agreed immediately.

When Jack returned, he went behind his house and saw something amazing. There was Esperanza, quietly talking to Luster. Luster was doing everything Jack had asked him to do! He was lying down, rolling over, stretching his paw towards Esperanza, and following her everywhere! Jack couldn't believe what he saw.

"What is going on?" he asked Esperanza.

"Oh, I'm just talking to your nice dog here!" Esperanza answered.

"But I have been trying to talk to him for the past eight weeks, and he won't do anything but sit! Now he is doing all kinds of things—and I'm supposed to be the expert dog trainer! What did you do?"

Esperanza laughed. "I am talking to this dog in Spanish! Someone must have spoken to Luster in Spanish when he was a puppy, because he understands it perfectly!"

"Well," said Jack, still very amazed. "That is really interesting. I guess you will have to teach me Spanish, Esperanza! It looks like Luster is going to be training me!"

## ✳ Thinking About the Story

### What Did You Understand?

A. Answer the following questions in complete sentences. Write your answers in the empty spaces. Then compare your answers with those of a classmate. Your teacher may wish to put these questions on the walls of your classroom and ask you to walk around with a partner answering the questions. Then each of you could take down one question and read it out loud, so that the whole class can talk about it.

1. Why do the police need dogs?

   _help fight crime — dog's can smell criminal's clothes for drugs_

2. How was Jack a good person for his job?

   _trained dogs_

3. Why was Jack disappointed with Luster?

   _impossible to train_

4. What surprised Jack so much?

   _when Luster did everything for Esperanza_

5. Why would Luster have to train Jack? _dog understood Spanish + he would have to help him_

118

B. Correct the sentences below according to the content of the story. Write your corrections in the blanks, and compare what you have written with a classmate.

1. Esperanza worked as a dog trainer.

   _Jack worked as a dog trainer_

2. Esperanza does not ~~speak~~ English. *understand*

   _____

3. Jack ~~doesn't~~ like Luster. *ed*

   _____ *brought to*

4. Luster was ~~lost~~ at the police department.

   _____

5. Luster was ~~not~~ really a smart dog. *who understood*
   _____ *Spanish*

## ❋ Working with Words

Match the words in Column A with their associations in Column B. Then compare your work with a classmate's work. Your answers may vary.

| Column A | Column B |
|----------|----------|
| police | hard work |
| expert | friend |
| training | find |
| patience | dogs |
| neighbor | owner |
| refuse | criminals |
| hide | law |
| belong | teacher |

119

## ❋ Working with Language

Jack says, "I have been trying to talk to him for weeks."
We say that we *have been* doing something when we talk about
an event that started in the past and continues into the present. Use
this form when you answer the questions below. Compare your
answers to those of a classmate. Your teacher might want you to ask
these questions and other such questions to your classmates.

1. How long have you been living in the place where you now live?

   I have been living here all my life

2. How long have you been studying English?

   I have been studyeng Eng

3. How long have you been sitting in your chair?

   I have been sitting

4. How long have you been studying English from this book?

   I have been studying

5. How long have you been practicing your pronunciation?

   I have been pract, my
   pronunceation

## ❋ Asking Questions

Following are answers to questions. Working with a partner,
decide what the questions are. Write your questions in the blank
spaces and compare your questions with those of other students.

1. What are poplul dogs used for ?

   Answer: The dogs help find criminals.

2. How long does it take to train a dog

   Answer: It takes a very long time to train a dog.

3. What is wrong w/Luster ?

   Answer: Because the dog looked smart and healthy.

4. _____ *Did Luster eventually listen to* [a obey] ? *Jack's commands*

Answer: Luster became more stubborn.

5. _____ *Did Luster like Esperanze* ?

Answer: He was following her everywhere.

## ❋ Rewriting the Story

Below is the story you just read, only now words are missing from it. Some of the blanks need only one word in them. Others need several words. First, fill in as many of the missing words as you can on your own. Then, working with a classmate, fill in the rest of the blanks to make the story complete. Check this story with the complete story.

## The Dog Who Spoke Spanish

JACK RUBIN was a 1. *policeman* who trained dogs. He trained big, smart dogs to help the Bridgeport Police Department find 2. *criminals*. Jack's dogs knew the smell of criminals. They also knew the smell of 3. *drugs*. When the dogs smelled a criminal's clothes, drugs, or something else that belonged to the criminal, they would follow the smell and lead policemen to where the criminal was hiding. Because of Jack's dogs, the police 4. _____ many dangerous drug smugglers.

It takes a lot of time and 5. _____ for Jack to train his dogs. Sometimes it is difficult for Jack to find the right kind of dog to train. One day, Frank Johnson, the town's mayor, brought a beautiful young dog to the police department. "I thought this dog might make a good 6. _____," Frank told Jack. "He seems very 7. _____."

Jack liked the dog, and he liked what he saw. The dog was big and healthy. Its 8. _____ was shiny, its eyes were bright, and it noticed everything. "He certainly looks just like the kind of

121

dog that I enjoy 9. _____. Where did you find him?" Jack asked.

"He has been wandering around my neighborhood for the past week, and I haven't been able to find his 10. _____," said Frank. "I've been 11. _____ him and thought you could use him."

The kind of dog Jack needed was usually very 12. _____, so Jack was happy to get this dog for free. Jack named the dog "Luster" since his coat was so 13. _____. Jack took Luster home and began training him.

After a few days, Jack realized that something 14. _____ with Luster. Though Luster was a nice dog and seemed to like Jack a lot, it was impossible to train him! No matter how hard Jack tried, Luster would not 15. _____ to his commands. Poor Jack! How could he ever train a dog that didn't listen? Jack just couldn't figure out what was wrong. He knew the dog wasn't 16. _____, so he kept trying to train him. But the more Jack worked with Luster, the 17. _____ Luster became. Most of the time, Luster just sat in front of Jack, wagging his tail and looking happy. Jack decided 18. _____. Luster would never be a police dog.

A week later, Jack had to leave town for a meeting. He asked Esperanza Lamas, his 19. _____, to take care of Luster. Esperanza loved dogs, so she 20. _____ immediately.

When Jack returned, he went behind his house and saw something 21. _____. There was Esperanza, quietly talking to Luster. Luster was doing everything Jack had asked him to do! He was lying down, rolling over, stretching his paw towards Esperanza, and 22. _____ her everywhere! Jack couldn't 23. _____ what he saw.

"What is going on?" he asked Esperanza.

"Oh, I'm just 24. _____ to your nice dog here!" Esperanza answered.

"But I have been trying to talk to him for the past eight weeks, and he won't do anything but sit! Now he is doing all kinds of things—and I'm supposed to be the 25. _____ dog trainer! What did you do?"

Esperanza laughed. "I am talking to this dog 26. _____! Someone must have spoken to Luster in Spanish when he was a puppy, because he 27. _____ it perfectly!"

"Well," said Jack, still very amazed. "That is really interesting. I guess you will have 28. _____ me Spanish, Esperanza! It looks like Luster is going to be 29. _____ me!"

## ✸ Retelling the Story

Working with a classmate, tell each other the story in your own words. Use the following words and expressions to help you.

> the Bridgeport Police Department
> criminals
> follow the smell
> coat was shiny
> Luster
> stubborn
> give up
> neighbor
> does all kinds of things
> Spanish

## ✳ Extending the Story

A. Animals have always been very important to people. In small groups, talk about the usefulness of animals. Use your own experiences whenever possible. Your teacher may ask you to write about some of these experiences.

B. Think about the people who live close to you (your neighbors). How many of them do you know? Do you live in a place where neighbors know one another? Do neighbors help one another?

C. Is drug smuggling a serious problem in your country? What do you think should be done about drugs in the world today? Talk about this problem in your group. Ask someone in the group to take notes, and tell the rest of the class what you have talked about. Then listen to and comment on what other groups have to say.

*Story 11*

# The Good Porter

## ❋ Before You Read

*Talking About the Picture*

Look at the picture. Then, with a partner, answer the questions below. When you have finished talking to your partner, tell the rest of the class what you decided. Listen to the ideas of the other students.

- Have you ever traveled by train? If you have, tell your classmates about the experience.
- Going by train is usually not the fastest way of getting somewhere. Still, some people love traveling by train. Why do you think that they like it so much?
- In your country, do people give tips for services? When do they tip? Do you think that tipping is a good custom?

Knowing the words below will help you to understand the story. Listen and repeat as your teacher reads the words. Do you know what these words mean? Ask your teacher or your classmates to help you if you need a meaning explained. Then read the story.

| | | | |
|---|---|---|---|
| porter | business | conference | dresser |
| railroad company | tip | polite | drawer |
| to appreciate | necessities | to behave | certificate |
| to support | dining car | nervous | worth |
| passengers | tablecloth | disappointed | generously |
| comfortable | to joke | | |

## ❋ The Story

# The Good Porter

DAVE HILLMAN worked as a porter in a large railroad company. He helped passengers carry their suitcases and feel as comfortable as possible. Dave's job didn't pay very much, but he usually made a little more money in tips. Most of the passengers would tip Dave as a way of saying thank you for everything he did. Dave always appreciated the tips he received; they made him feel good about being a porter and helping people.

More than anything, though, Dave needed the tips to support his family. He always wanted his wife, Mary, and his children, Linda and Steven, to have the best of things. Mary needed a new washing machine, and Linda and Steven both wanted bicycles. It was difficult to buy them what they wanted, as Dave's money was quickly spent on food, clothes, and other necessities. So Dave worked especially hard as a porter, hoping that he could make more money.

One day Dave's boss asked him to go on a very long train trip. Dave would be gone for many weeks. He didn't want to leave his family for that long, but he also knew that many rich

businesspeople would be on this train. He hoped that if he gave
these businesspeople good service, he would get very large tips. [20]
Dave said good-bye to Mary, Linda, and Steven before boarding
the train.

In New York, ten very successful businesspeople got on the
train. Dave carried their luggage and helped them find their seats.
The businesspeople were going to Denver, Colorado, for a big [25]
conference. Each day, Dave brushed their suits, polished their shoes,
and brought them fresh coffee and rolls in the morning. He saw to
it that they had a special table for ten in the dining car, that there
was always a clean, white tablecloth on their table, and that there
were fresh flowers in their sleeping cars. He made sure their food [30]
was hot, their wine was cold, and their desserts were delicious. The
business people laughed and joked with Dave. They told him how
much they enjoyed the train ride and how comfortable he made it
for them to sit and talk about business deals. Dave thought they
were wonderful! He thought of the money he would get in tips and [35]
dreamed of all the things he could buy his family. In his dreams,
there was a shiny new washing machine and two bright red bicycles.

Before Dave knew it, the train arrived in Denver. The trip
went so fast! Dave felt sad that it was over. He carried all the
business people's suitcases off the train. Then he stood at the door [40]
to shake hands with each of them. The first businessperson got
off. She shook Dave's hand and warmly said, "Dave, you have
been a wonderful porter. It was a great trip. Thank you." But she
did not leave a tip. The second businessperson got off the train.
He shook Dave's hand warmly and said, "Dave, I have never met a [45]
porter as good as you." But he didn't leave a tip. The third
businessperson got off the train. He shook Dave's hand warmly
and said, "It was such a comfortable trip, Dave, and it's all because
of you." But this businessman did not leave a tip. The next six
people in the business group behaved in the same way. They were [50]
all very polite, and they all thanked Dave, but no one left a tip.
Dave was feeling sad and nervous. Finally, Mrs. Smith, the tenth
businessperson, got off the train.

"Dave," she said, "you have been an excellent porter. Thank you for making our journey such a pleasant one. We have all decided to give you this." She handed Dave a very strange piece of paper, but she gave him no money.

Dave felt sad and disappointed. He went home and put the paper in a drawer. He would have to wait many more years before he could buy a washing machine for Mary and bicycles for Linda and Steven.

Dave worked hard for many years. Linda and Steven were both in high school, and now they wanted to go to college. Dave still didn't have enough money for a washing machine and bicycles, and he certainly didn't have enough money to send Linda and Steven to college! Dave was very depressed.

One day, Mary was looking in their dresser when she found a strange piece of paper in the bottom drawer. She took the paper out and unfolded it. It was a stock certificate for a telephone company. Mary asked Dave about the paper. Dave remembered the day he came home from the train trip to Denver. He remembered that he was upset because the businesspeople had only given him a piece of paper for a tip. He had put the paper in the drawer and forgotten about it. He never thought the piece of paper was worth something. Mary knew that the prices of stocks were listed in newspapers. She bought a newspaper and looked up the phone company's stock. She couldn't believe what she read—the stock certificate was worth one million dollars! Dave finally had enough money to buy a washing machine for Mary and bicycles for Linda and Steven. He also sent Linda and Steven to very good colleges.

Now Dave and Mary live in a house by a beach in California. Sometimes they go on trips. They always take the train, and they always tip the porters generously.

# ✳ Thinking About the Story

*What Did You Understand?*

A. Answer the following questions in complete sentences. Write your answers in the empty spaces. Then compare your answers with those of a classmate. Your teacher may wish to put these questions on the walls of your classroom and ask you to walk around with a partner answering the questions. Then each of you could take down one question and read it out loud, so that the whole class can talk about it.

1. Why was Dave happy that rich businesspeople were going to ride his train?

   _____

2. What did Dave do for the businesspeople?

   _____

3. Why did Dave need the tips?

   _____

4. Who is Linda?

   _____

5. Why was Dave sad when the train arrived in Colorado?

   _____

6. Why was Dave so disappointed?

   _____

7. How was the strange paper discovered?

   _____

8. What was the surprise?

   _____

B. Correct the sentences below according to the content of the story. Write your corrections in the blanks and compare what you have written with a classmate.

1. Dave did not enjoy his trip with the businesspeople.

_____

2. The businesspeople were not very generous.

_____

3. Dave always wanted things for himself.

_____

4. Dave had always planned to send his children to college.

_____

5. Mary cried because she didn't get a washing machine.

_____

## ❋ Working with Words

The word *porter* comes into English from French and means *to carry.* A porter carries suitcases for travelers. Other words from the root, *port,* are *import* (carry something into a country), *export* (carry something out of a country), *deportment* (the way a person carries him or herself), and *report* (carry something again—that is to carry news by describing something that you heard about).

The following sentences using words with the root *port* have been started for you. Finish them in any way you want and read your sentences to a classmate. Then listen to your classmate's sentences.

1. The porter took my suitcase when

_____.

2. My country imports

_____.

3. My country exports

_____.

4. I had to report to my father when

_____.

## ❋ Working with Language

Match the beginning of the sentences in Column A with the correct endings in Column B. Then read the completed sentences to a classmate.

*Column A*

Dave was very excited

Mary needed a washing machine

Dave's two children wanted to go to college,

The businesspeople had a very good time on the train,

Mary found a strange piece of paper in a drawer,

Dave and Mary always tip the porters generously

*Column B*

but there was not enough money to send them.

but they didn't leave any tips.

and she decided to check whether it was worth anything.

and Dave really wanted to buy one for her.

when they go on trips.

when he heard that some very rich businesspeople were going to ride the train.

## ✵ Asking Questions

Following are answers to questions. Working with a partner, decide what the questions are. Write your questions in the blank spaces and compare your questions with those of other students.

1. _____?

    Answer: A washing machine.

2. _____?

    Answer: Dave brushed their suits, polished their shoes, and brought them fresh coffee and rolls in the morning.

3. _____?

    Answer: He dreamed of all the things he could buy his family.

4. _____?

    Answer: The businesspeople did not leave any tips.

5. _____?

    Answer: A strange piece of paper.

## ✵ Rewriting the Story

Below is the story you just read, only now words are missing from it. Some of the blanks need only one word in them. Others need several words. First, fill in as many of the missing words as you can on your own. Then, working with a classmate, fill in the rest of the blanks to make the story complete. Check this story with the complete story.

## *The Good Porter*

DAVE HILLMAN worked as a porter in a large railroad company. He helped passengers carry their 1. _____ and feel as 2. _____ as possible. Dave's job didn't pay very much, but he usually made a little more money in tips. Most of the passengers would tip Dave as a way of saying 3. _____ for everything he did. Dave always appreciated the tips he received; they made him feel good about being a porter and helping people.

More than anything, though, Dave needed the tips 4. _____ his family. He always wanted his wife, Mary, and his children, Linda and Steven, to have the 5. _____ of things. Mary needed a new 6. _____, and Linda and Steven both wanted bicycles. It was difficult to buy them what they wanted, as Dave's money was quickly spent on food, clothes, and other 7. _____. So Dave worked especially hard as a porter, hoping that he could make more money.

One day Dave's boss asked him to go on a very long train trip. Dave would be gone for many weeks. He didn't want to leave his family for that long, but he also knew that many rich businesspeople would be on this train. He hoped that if he gave these businesspeople good service, he would get very large tips. Dave said good-bye to Mary, Linda, and Steven before boarding the train.

In New York, ten very 8. _____ businesspeople got on the train. Dave carried their luggage and helped them find their seats. The businesspeople were going to Denver, Colorado, for a big 9. _____. Each day, Dave brushed their suits, polished their shoes, and brought them fresh coffee and rolls in the morning. He saw to it that they had a special table for ten in the dining car, that there was always a clean, white tablecloth on their table, and that there were fresh 10. _____ in their sleeping cars. He made sure their food was hot, their wine was cold, and their desserts were delicious. The businesspeople 11. _____ and joked with Dave. They told him how much they enjoyed the train ride and how comfortable he made it for them to sit and talk about business deals. Dave thought they were 12. _____! He thought of the money he would get in tips and 13. _____ of all the things he could buy his family. In his dreams, there was a shiny new washing machine and two bright red 14. _____.

Before Dave knew it, the train 15. _____ in Denver. The trip went so fast! Dave felt sad that it was over. He carried all the businesspeople's suitcases off the train. Then he stood at the door 16. _____ hands with each of them. The first businessperson got off. She shook Dave's hand and warmly said, "Dave, you have been a wonderful porter. It was a great trip. Thank you." But she did not 17. _____ a tip. The second businessperson got off the train. He shook Dave's hand warmly and said, "Dave, I have never met a porter as good as you." But he didn't leave a tip. The third businessperson got off the train. He 18. _____ Dave's hand warmly and said, "It was such a comfortable trip, Dave, and it's all because of you." But this businessman did not leave a tip. The next six people in the business group behaved in the same way. They were all very polite, and they all thanked Dave, but no one left a tip. Dave was 19. _____ sad and nervous. Finally, Mrs. Smith, the tenth businessperson, got off the train.

"Dave," she said, "you have been an excellent porter. Thank you for making our journey such a pleasant one. We have all decided 20. _____ you this." She handed Dave a very 21. _____ piece of paper, but she gave him no money.

Dave felt sad and 22. _____. He went home and put the paper in a 23. _____. He would have to wait many more years before he could buy a washing machine for Mary and bicycles for Linda and Steven.

Dave worked hard for many years. Linda and Steven were both in high school, and now they wanted to go to 24. _____. Dave still didn't have enough money for a washing machine and bicycles, and he certainly didn't have 25. _____ money to send Linda and Steven to college! Dave was very depressed.

One day, Mary was looking in their 26. _____ when

134

she found a strange piece of paper in the bottom drawer. She took the paper out and unfolded it. It was a stock 27. _____ for a telephone company. Mary asked Dave about the paper. Dave remembered the day he came home from the train trip to Denver. He remembered that he was upset because the businesspeople had only given him a piece of paper for a tip. He had put the paper in the drawer and 28. _____ about it. He never thought the piece of paper was 29. _____ something. Mary knew that the prices of stocks were listed in newspapers. She bought a newspaper and looked up the phone company's stock. She couldn't believe what she read—the stock certificate was worth one million dollars! Dave finally had enough money to buy a washing machine for Mary and bicycles for Linda and Steven. He also sent Linda and Steven to very good colleges.

Now Dave and Mary live in a house by a 30. _____ in California. Sometimes they go on trips. They always take the train, and they always tip the porters 31. _____.

## ❋ Retelling the Story

Working with a classmate, tell each other the story in your own words. Use the following words and expressions to help you.

| | |
|---|---|
| porter | enjoyed the ride |
| tips | dreamed |
| support his family | shook hands |
| washing machine | disappointed |
| bicycles | worked many years |
| businesspeople | strange piece of paper |
| best table | stock certificate |
| shined shoes | one million |
| fresh flowers | tips the porters generously |

135

## ✳ Extending the Story

A. All of us have big disappointments in life. There are things we hoped for and expected that didn't come true. These disappointments make people sad and frustrated, but sometimes, like in Dave's case, the disappointment turns into something very good. Do you remember a situation in which something disappointing turned into something good? Think of a situation in your own life or in the life of someone you know, heard about, or read about. In small groups, tell your classmates your story and listen to their stories. Your teacher might ask you to turn these stories into writing assignments.

B. Dave wants to buy his wife, Mary, a washing machine. This machine is very important to Mary. Below is a list of things that are important in people's lives today. Choose the mechanical device that is of greatest importance to you, and in small groups, explain to your classmates why it is important. Next, prioritize the devices; that is, list them in order of importance in your life. Then compare your list with a partner's and try to come to an agreement on the order of importance.

> a washing machine
> a clothes dryer
> a VCR
> a computer
> an answering machine
> a telephone
> a television
> a popcorn popper
> a kitchen stove
> an electric frying pan
> a coffeemaker
> a refrigerator
> a vacuum cleaner

# The Boy Who Used Logic

## ✸ Before You Read

*Talking About the Picture*

Look at the picture. Then, with a partner, answer the questions below. When you have finished talking to your partner, tell the rest of the class what you decided. Listen to the ideas of the other students.

- Who do you think the people in the picture are?
- Do you think that they eat together every day? Why or why not?
- How old do you think these people are?
- How do you think each person is feeling?
- Who do you think is talking the most? Why?

137

Knowing the words below will help you to understand the story. Listen and repeat as your teacher reads the words. Do you know what these words mean? Ask your teacher or your classmates to help you if you need a meaning explained. Then read the story.

| | |
|---|---|
| to educate | patient |
| sports | attitude |
| to accept | logic |
| to miss someone | to be fed up with something |
| to change | beet |
| conceited | intelligent |
| confident | ashamed |
| to be impressed with yourself | to hug |

## ✳ The Story

# The Boy Who Used Logic

MR. AND MRS. NORTON lived in a small town called Bonville by the Mississippi river. Though neither of them had gone to college, they had always wanted their only son, George, to have a good education. Ever since the day George was born, Mr. and Mrs. Norton worked hard to educate him. They taught him all they knew, helped him with his homework, and supported him in all the sports he played. You can imagine how proud they were when George was accepted into one of the top colleges in the United States. When George left, they held a good-bye party for him and wished him much success.

In December, when George returned home for the holidays, his parents were very excited to see him. They had missed him a lot and wanted to know all about his days at college. But George had changed, and the changes were not what Mr. and Mrs. Norton expected. George had become very conceited. He thought he was the smartest person in Bonville and told everyone how good he was in college. He treated his parents as if they were stupid just because they didn't know the things he had learned at the university.

Mr. Norton was very upset with his son. "Maybe we did the wrong thing when we decided to send him to the university," he told his wife. "George has become such a conceited young man." 20

Mrs. Norton was not as worried. "Don't be so angry," she told her husband. "George is just young, confident, and impressed with himself because he has been out in the big world. You must give him some time to grow up. Be patient." 25

One evening when the family was eating dinner, George suddenly said, "Let me show you what I have learned about logic at the university."

Mr. Norton was a bit tired of George's attitude, but he remembered what Mrs. Norton had said and tried to be patient. 30

"How many chickens are we having for dinner tonight?" George proudly asked his parents.

"Two chickens," said his mother.

"No," said George. "I will show you with university logic that we are really having three chickens." 35

His parents didn't say anything. They just waited.

"Here," said George, and he put his fork into one chicken. "Here is chicken one." Then George put his fork into the second chicken and said, "Here is chicken two!" He laughed as if he were the smartest person in the whole wide world and 40 said, "One and two are three—so you see we are really having three chickens for dinner!"

By now Mr. Norton was pretty fed up with George's "know it all" behavior. He couldn't be patient anymore, so he turned to his wife and said, "This logic is wonderful! Aren't we glad that we 45 sent George away to learn this important stuff! You can have chicken one for your dinner, I'll have chicken two, and George, who has gotten to be so smart, can eat the third chicken."

There was silence at the table. George knew that his "logic" was really wrong, and his face turned red as a beet. 50 Suddenly he understood how silly he had been acting. He realized that his parents were intelligent people even though they had not gone to college. George felt ashamed of himself. He got up from the table and hugged his parents. "Thank you for being such wonderful parents!" he said. That was the best logic they had heard for a long time.

55

## ❋ Thinking About the Story

### *What Did You Understand?*

Answer the following questions in complete sentences. Write your answers in the empty spaces. Then compare your answers with those of a classmate. Your teacher may wish to put these questions on the walls of your classroom and ask you to walk around with a partner answering the questions. Then each of you could take down one question and read it out loud, so that the whole class can talk about it.

1. Why were the Nortons proud?

   _____

2. What kind of person was George before he went to college?

   _____

3. How did George's parents feel when he left for the university? (Give two feelings.)

   _____

   _____

4. How did George's parents feel when George returned?

   _____

5. Why was Mr. Norton upset?

   _____

6. Why was Mr. Norton fed up?

_____

7. Why did George's face turn red?

_____

## ❋ Working with Words

Working in small groups or in pairs, finish the sentences below any way you wish. Read your sentences to the whole class and listen to the sentences of other groups.

1. When George went to the university, he

_____.

2. The Nortons were proud of their son because

_____.

3. George thought he could impress his parents by

_____.

4. Parents sometimes have to be patient with their children because

_____.

5. Children sometimes have to be patient with their parents because

_____.

6. In some cultures people eat with knives, spoons, and forks, but in other cultures

_____.

7. George felt ashamed because

_____.

8. When George hugged his parents, they

_____.

9. George realized that his parents were smart because

_____.

## ❈ Working with Language

### The Past Perfect Tense

A. Read the sentences below carefully. Notice that each sentence uses the verb *had* together with the main verb. We use this form (the past perfect) when there are two actions in the past and one action comes before another. The action that happens first uses the main verb together with *had*.

Working with a partner, circle the first action and underline the second in each sentence. Then check your results with the rest of the class.

1. George had always been a good boy who was very close to his parents.

2. When George returned home, his parents noticed that he had become very proud.

3. George treated his parents as if they were very stupid because they had not learned the things he had learned at the university.

4. Suddenly George understood how silly he had been acting when he made his parents feel bad.

B. In the sentences below, write the correct form of the verb in the blank spaces.

1. When George (to come) _____ home, he wanted to tell everyone about the things that he (to learn) _____ at the university.

2. Mr. and Mrs. Norton wondered if they (to do) _____ the right thing when they (to decide) _____ to send George to the university.

3. When everyone (to finish) _____ eating dinner, they started to talk.

4. I (to do) _____ my homework when the teacher asked me about it.

5. We (to clean) _____ the house before the guests (to come ) _____.

## ✿ Asking Questions

Following are answers to questions. Working with a partner, decide what the questions are. Write your questions in the blank spaces and compare your questions with those of other students.

1. _____?
   Answer: In a small town.

2. _____?
   Answer: Two chickens.

3. _____?
   Answer: Because he felt ashamed.

4. _____?

Answer: During the holidays.

5. _____?

Answer: He got up from the table.

## ❋ Rewriting the Story

Below is the story you just read, only now words are missing from it. Some of the blanks need only one word in them. Others need several words. First, fill in as many of the missing words as you can on your own. Then, working with a classmate, fill in the rest of the blanks to make the story complete. Check this story with the complete story.

# *The Boy Who Used Logic*

Mr. and Mrs. Norton 1. _____ in a small town called Bonville by the Mississippi river. Though neither of them had gone to college, they had always wanted their only son, George, to have a good 2. _____. Ever since the day George was born, Mr. and Mrs. Norton worked hard 3. _____ him. They taught him all they knew, helped him with his homework, and supported him in all the 4. _____ he played. You can imagine how proud they were when George was 5. _____ into one of the top colleges in the United States. When George left, they held a good-bye party for him and wished him much success.

In December, when George 6. _____ home for the holidays, his parents were very excited to see him. They 7. _____ him a lot and wanted to know all about his days at college. But George 8. _____, and the changes were not what Mr. and Mrs. Norton expected. George had become very 9. _____. He thought he was the smartest person in

144

Bonville and told everyone how good he was in college. He treated his parents as if they were stupid just because they didn't know the things he 10. _____ at the university.

Mr. Norton was very upset with his son. "Maybe we did the wrong thing when we decided to send him to the university," he told his wife. "George has become such a conceited young man."

Mrs. Norton was not as worried. "Don't be so angry," she told her husband. "George is just young, confident, and 11. _____ with himself because he has been out in the big world. You must give him some time 12. _____ up. Be 13. _____."

One evening when the family was eating dinner, George suddenly said, "Let me show you what I have learned about logic at the university."

Mr. Norton was a bit tired of George's 14. _____, but he remembered what Mrs. Norton had said and tried to be patient.

"How many 15. _____ are we having for dinner tonight?" George proudly asked his parents.

"Two chickens," said his mother.

"No," said George. "I will show you with university 16. _____ that we are really having three chickens."

His parents didn't say anything. They just waited.

"Here," said George, and he put his fork into one chicken. "Here is chicken one." Then George put his fork into the second chicken and said, "Here is chicken two!" He laughed as if he were the 17. _____ person in the whole wide world and said, "One and two are three—so you see we are really having three chickens for dinner!"

By now Mr. Norton was pretty 18. _____ with George's "know it all" behavior. He couldn't be patient anymore, so he turned to his wife and said, "This logic is wonderful! Aren't we glad that we sent George away 19. _____ this important stuff! You can have chicken one for your dinner, I'll have chicken

145

two, and George, who has gotten to be so smart, can eat the third chicken."

There was silence at the table. George knew that his "logic" was really wrong, and his face turned red as a 20. _____. Suddenly he understood how silly he had been acting. He realized that his parents were 21. _____ people even though they had not gone to college. George felt 22. _____ of himself. He got up from the table and 23. _____ his parents. "Thank you for being such wonderful parents!" he said. That was the best 24. _____ they had heard for a long time.

## ❋ Retelling the Story

Working with a classmate, tell each other the story in your own words. Use the following words and expressions to help you.

| | |
|---|---|
| Bonville | dinner |
| gone to college | chickens |
| missed him very much | red as a beet |
| conceited | ashamed |
| logic | hugged |

## ❋ Extending the Story

A. Below are names given to some of the paragraphs in the story. Working with a partner, decide which paragraph fits each name the best. Tell the class about your decisions and listen to what other groups have decided.

University Logic
George Has Changed!
Be Patient!
Pride
Wonderful Logic
Shame

B. Mark Twain, a very famous American writer, once said that when he was fourteen years old, he thought that his father didn't know anything. Then when he became twenty-one years old, he was surprised at how much the old man had learned in seven years.

In small groups, discuss how what Mark Twain said is related to the story you read and to people's lives. Ask one person in your group to take notes. Share your ideas with the whole class.

Story 13

# Do What Your Heart Asks For

## ❋ Before You Read

*Talking About the Picture*

Look at the picture. Then, with a partner, answer the questions below. When you have finished talking to your partner, tell the rest of the class what you decided. Listen to the ideas of the other students.

- Why is it important to bring babies to the doctor?
- Does the doctor in the picture look happy?
- Does the mother look happy?
- Do you think the baby likes the doctor?
- How long do you think the man in the picture has been a doctor?

Knowing the words below will help you to understand the story. Listen and repeat as your teacher reads the words. Do you know what these words mean? Ask your teacher or your classmates to help you if you need a meaning explained. Then read the story.

| | |
|---|---|
| to treat | pediatrician |
| respected | bitter |
| frustrated | counselor |
| pharmacies | to suggest |
| medical school | to apply |
| patients | to dedicate |
| to afford | to practice medicine |

## ✵ The Story

## Do What Your Heart Asks For

WILLIAM JAMES was fifty years old and a very successful businessman. He was the owner of a bottle capping company that made a great deal of money. Many people worked in his company, and they all liked the way William treated them.

William had a very nice wife, a son, and two daughters. His children were very intelligent, and his wife was a respected lawyer. He loved his family and always remembered to tell them how much he cared. They lived in a large, brick house with a lovely garden behind it.

William seemed like a very happy man, but inside he felt unhappy and frustrated. When William was a young man, he had wanted to be a doctor with all his heart. He studied medical books and learned about how the human body works. He went to hospitals and pharmacies to talk to the doctors and visit the patients. He loved to help people who were sick, but he had one big problem: he couldn't afford to go to medical school. Medical school

150

was expensive, and William's family was very poor. His father had died when William was sixteen years old. William was forced to work at the bottle capping factory to make money for his mother and sister. William worked and worked until he owned the factory and had a lot of money, but he felt that he had wasted his life doing work that he didn't really like.

The more William thought about it, the more bitter and angry he became. His wife knew that something was wrong, and she suggested he go to a counselor to get help.

The counselor listened carefully to William talk about his feelings. When William was finished, the counselor shook his head. "I don't understand your problem, William. Today you have plenty of money. Your factory can work without you and still make money. Why don't you go to medical school now and become a doctor just as you have always wanted?"

William couldn't believe what the counselor was telling him. "Are you crazy?" he asked. "I am fifty years old. How can I possibly go to school now? Why, I would have to learn the most basic of things! It would take me at least ten years to become a doctor. I would be at least sixty years old before I finished!"

"Yes," said the counselor. "And please tell me how old you are going to be in ten years if you don't go to medical school?"

Suddenly William understood. He shook the counselor's hand and thanked him. Then he went home to apply for medical school.

Eight years later, William became a pediatrician. He sold his factory and dedicated himself to being the best doctor in town. All of his patients liked him, and he was a very happy man.

William practiced medicine until he was seventy-five years old. One day his son came home from his job at a bank. He was upset and worried. "Dad," he said. "I have a problem. I really want to be a teacher, but the bank wants me to keep working there. What should I do?" William sat back in his chair and smiled. "Son," he said, "Do what your heart asks for."

# ✸ Thinking About the Story

*What Did You Understand?*

Answer the following questions in complete sentences. Write your answers in the empty spaces. Then compare your answers with those of a classmate. Your teacher may wish to put these questions on the walls of your classroom and ask you to walk around with a partner answering the questions. Then each of you could take down one question and read it out loud so that the whole class can talk about it.

1. What kind of work did William do when he was young?

_____

2. What did William study when he was a boy?

_____

3. Why didn't William go to medical school when he was young?

_____

4. What did William say when he heard the counselor's suggestion?

_____

5. What was the counselor's answer?

_____

6. Why did William sell his factory?

_____

7. Why was William a happy man?

_____

8. What did William tell his son?

_____

## ✳ Working with Words

A. Match the words in the first column with their definitions in the second column. Work on your own. Then compare your results with a partner.

1. _____ successful
2. _____ owner
3. _____ frustrated
4. _____ factory
5. _____ medicine
6. _____ pediatrician
7. _____ expensive
8. _____ plenty
9. _____ bitter
10. _____ outstanding

a. the opposite of cheap
b. a lot
c. the opposite of sweet
d. excellent
e. doing well in life
f. someone who has something that belongs to him/her
g. unhappy because you cannot do what you want to do
h. place where things are made
i. something you take when you are sick
j. doctor for children

B. In the story there are many words that describe good feelings, and there are other words that describe bad feelings. Working with a classmate, find the words in the story that belong in these columns. Write them in the right place on the chart. You may also write words that are not in the story.

When you have finished your chart, compare it with the charts of other students in your class. The first two words have been done for you.

| Positive Words | Negative Words |
| --- | --- |
| *successful* | *unhappy* |
| | |
| | |
| | |
| | |
| | |
| | |

## ❋ Working with Language

An *adjective* is a word that describes a person or a thing. There are many adjectives in the story that you have read. Below is a list of adjectives from the story. Working with a partner, find the person or thing that each adjective describes. When you have finished your list, compare it with your classmates' lists. The first two words have been done for you.

1. successful     businessman
2. nice     wife
3. intelligent     _____
4. respected     _____
5. lovely     _____

6. large      _____

7. brick      _____

8. unhappy      _____

9. frustrated      _____

10. sick      _____

11. expensive      _____

12. poor      _____

13. medical      _____

14. bitter      _____

15. angry      _____

16. wrong      _____

17. crazy      _____

18. basic      _____

19. best      _____

20. worried      _____

## ✳ Asking Questions

Following are answers to questions. Working with a partner, decide what the questions are. Write your questions in the blank spaces and compare your questions with those of other students.

1. _____?

Answer: Fifty years old.

2. _____?

Answer: He worked in a factory.

3. _____?

Answer: He couldn't afford to go to medical school.

4. _____?

Answer: "Go to school now."

5. _____?

Answer: Eight years.

## ✸ Rewriting the Story

Below is the story you just read, only now words are missing from it. Some of the blanks need only one word in them. Others need several words. First, fill in as many of the missing words as you can on your own. Then, working with a classmate, fill in the rest of the blanks to make the story complete. Check this story with the complete story.

## *Do What Your Heart Asks For*

WILLIAM JAMES was fifty years old and a very successful 1. _____. He was the owner of a bottle capping company that made a great deal of money. Many people worked in his company, and they all liked the way William 2. _____ them.

William had a very nice wife, a son, and two daughters. His children were very intelligent, and his wife was a respected lawyer. He loved his family and always 3. _____ to tell them how much he cared. They lived in a large, brick house with a lovely garden 4._____ it.

William seemed like a very happy man, but inside he felt unhappy and frustrated. When William was a young man, he had wanted to be a 5. _____ with all his heart. He studied medical books and learned about how the human body works. He went to hospitals and 6. _____ to talk to the doctors and visit the patients. He loved to help people who were sick, but he had one big problem: he couldn't 7. _____ to go to medical school. Medical school was expensive, and William's family was very poor. His father had died when William was sixteen years old. William was forced 8. _____ at the bottle capping factory 9._____ for his mother and sister. William worked and worked until he owned the factory and had a lot of money, but he felt that he had 10. _____ his life doing work that he didn't really like. The more William thought about it, the more bitter and angry he became. His wife knew that something was 11. _____, and she suggested he go to a 12. _____ to get help.

The counselor listened 13. _____ to William talk about his feelings. When William was finished, the counselor shook his head. "I don't understand your problem, William. Today you have 14. _____ money. Your factory can work without you and still make money. Why don't you go to medical school now and become a doctor just as you have 15. _____ wanted?"

William couldn't believe what the counselor was telling him. "Are you crazy?" he asked. "I am fifty years old. How can I possibly go to school now? Why, I would have to learn the most basic of things! It would take me at least 16. _____ to become a doctor. I would be at least sixty years old before I 17. _____!"

"Yes," said the counselor. "And please tell me how 18. _____ you are going to be in ten years if you don't go to medical school?"

Suddenly William understood. He shook the counselor's hand and thanked him. Then he went home 19. _____ for medical school.

Eight years 20. _____, William became a pediatrician. He sold his factory and 21. _____ himself to being the best doctor in town. All of his patients liked him, and he was a very happy man.

William practiced medicine until he was seventy-five years old. One day his son came home from his job at a bank. He was upset and worried. "Dad," he said. "I have a 22. _____. I really want to be a teacher, but the bank wants me to keep working there. What should I do?" William sat back in his chair and smiled. "Son," he said, "Do what your heart 23. _____."

157

## ✤ Retelling the Story

Below are first sentences from each paragraph in the story. Working with a classmate, see if you can tell each other the story. Use the sentences to help you.

1. William James was fifty years old and a very successful businessman.

2. William had a very nice wife, a son, and two daughters.

3. William seemed like a very happy man, but inside he felt unhappy and frustrated.

4. The counselor listened carefully to William talk about his feelings.

5. William couldn't believe what the counselor was telling him.

6. "Yes," said the counselor.

7. Suddenly William understood.

8. Eight years later, William became a pediatrician.

9. William practiced medicine until he was seventy-five years old.

## ✤ Extending the Story

A. Following are questions for you and a small group of classmates. Talk about these questions and ask a person in your group to take notes. Then ask one person in your group to tell the rest of the class what you have decided. Listen to what other groups have to say.

1. What are some very important decisions people have to make in their lives?

2. Why is it hard to make some decisions?

3. Try to remember a decision that you made that was important. Are you happy with the decision that you made?

B. William decided to go to school when he was rather old. Do you think that there is a "right" age for everything?

Following are questions for you to discuss with your classmates in small groups. Ask one person in your group to take notes and later tell the class about your discussion.

1. When is the best time to get married? Why?

2. When is the best time to decide on your profession? Why?

3. When is the best time to have children? Why?

4. When is the best time to move out of your parents' home? Why?

5. What is the lesson of the story *Do What Your Heart Asks For?* Do you agree with this lesson? Why or why not?

# Martha's Many Cats

## ✳ Before You Read

*Talking About the Picture*

Look at the picture. Then, with a partner, answer the questions below. When you have finished talking to your partner, tell the rest of the class what you decided. Listen to the ideas of the other students.

- Where do you think the baby and the cats are?
- Do you think that these cats should be around the baby? Why or why not?
- Have you ever had a pet? How do you feel about pets?
- Do you think that it is good for children to have pets?

Knowing the words below will help you to understand the story. Listen and repeat as your teacher reads the words. Do you know what these words mean? Ask your teacher or your classmates to help you if you need a meaning explained. Then read the story.

| | | |
|---|---|---|
| to gather | cold | to sniff |
| bowl | stocking cap | ice |
| courthouse | cutest | to shake |
| lawyer | to twitch | to freeze |
| research | get rid | to stretch |
| gorgeous | to smother | to curl |

## ❋ The Story

## *Martha's Many Cats*

MARTHA KOWALSKI loved cats. She lived alone in a big house filled with cats. Her favorite cats were Attila, Napoleon, and Cuddles. Each cat had his or her own bowl to drink from. The name of each cat was written on his or her bowl, and Martha used to say that her cats knew how to read 5 because none of them would ever drink milk from another cat's bowl. Martha's cats were her family. When she came home from work in the evening, the cats would gather around her. She would pet them, feed them special food, and call them her babies.

Martha worked at the town's courthouse. She helped lawyers 10 research their cases. One day, she met Lennie O'Conner. Lennie was a new lawyer. He was tall and handsome, with dark brown eyes and a gorgeous smile. When he saw Martha, it was love at first sight. He asked her out for dinner, and soon they were going to all kinds of places together. 15

One day Lennie and Martha were walking in the park. It was very cold. They both had coats and stocking caps on, and they were walking very close to each other to stay warm. As they walked, Martha talked about her cats. "Attila has the cutest nose! It always twitches right when she is about to eat, and Napolean never sleeps! Cuddles always needs a hug—" 20

"You like your cats better than you like me!" Lennie interrupted. "All you talk about is your cats! Cuddles does this, and Napolean does that!" Lennie was upset.

"I'm sorry, Lennie." Martha didn't know what to do. "I know 25 I talk about my cats a lot, but they are very important to me. My cats are like family to me." Lennie listened to Martha talk. He didn't like cats, but he loved Martha, and he knew he would have to like her cats.

Soon Martha and Lennie got married. They moved into a 30 new house, and Martha brought all her cats. There were so many! Black ones, brown ones, yellow ones, gray ones . . . Lennie felt like they were everywhere! Sometimes he got mad at the cats, but he was very patient and learned to live with them. Then one day Martha came home with a big smile on her face. "Lennie!" she shouted, 35 very excited. "I'm going to have a baby!"

Lennie was very happy about the news, but he was also very worried. He knew that cats were not good to have around babies. They slept on top of babies and sometimes smothered them until they died! Lennie told Martha that she would have to 40 get rid of her cats.

Martha was very sad. She was going to have a baby, but the cats had been her babies for a long time. "Please, Lennie," she said. "Our cats are so smart. I'm sure that they won't hurt our baby." Lennie thought and thought about it. Finally he agreed that the cats 45 could stay awhile longer.

Kathleen was born in January. She was a beautiful baby girl, with blue eyes and red hair. The cats sniffed at Kathleen, but they didn't think she was much fun. They soon left her alone. Kathleen grew bigger, and she played a lot with the cats. Soon Kathleen started 50 going to school. Since her parents worked long hours, Kathleen often arrived home first. She fed the cats, talked to the cats, and treated the cats like part of her family, just like Martha did.

One day Kathleen came home from school and realized that she had lost her key to the house. Her parents wouldn't be home from work for another hour, and Kathleen was really scared. It was snowing and very cold. Kathleen didn't know where to go, so she sat down on the porch to wait. Her fingers felt like ice, and her whole body was shaking from the cold. She felt like she would freeze right there on the porch. Then Napolean came out of the cat door onto the porch. He sat on Kathleen, his body soft and warm. Then Cuddles came and stretched himself out by Napolean. Then Attila curled up by Cuddles. Soon all the cats were gathered around Kathleen. Some were sitting on her, some were lying by her, and some were curled up around her feet. They kept Kathleen warm and happy.

When Lennie came home, Kathleen was asleep on the porch with all the cats around her. Once they found out what happened, Martha laughed. "See, Lennie! Cats don't smother children—they keep them warm inside!" And never again did Lennie tell Martha that she couldn't have cats.

## ✸ Thinking About the Story

*What Did You Understand?*

Answer the following questions in complete sentences. Write your answers in the empty spaces. Then compare your answers with those of a classmate. Your teacher may wish to put these questions on the walls of your classroom and ask you to walk around with a partner answering the questions. Then each of you could take down one question and read it out loud so that the whole class can talk about it.

1. Why did Martha think that her cats knew how to read?

_____

2. How did Lennie feel about cats?

_____

3. Why did Lennie change his mind?

_____

4. When did Lennie change his mind again?

_____

5. How did the cats feel about the baby?

_____

6. How did Kathleen feel about the cats?

_____

7. What happened to Kathleen?

_____

8. Why did Lennie never again tell Martha that she couldn't have cats?

_____

# ❋ Working with Words

A. Match the beginning of the sentence in Column A with the correct ending in Column B. Then read the completed sentences to a classmate.

*Column A*

When a lawyer defends someone,

He is a very famous artist in our country

Don't be so jealous when

Your bowl is too small

I was very surprised when

People always meet and talk

When it snows outside

That scarf is choking you

If you get rid of these important papers

My mother was angry

*Column B*

for this much soup.

my friends gave a party for me.

in our office.

we wear our stocking caps.

because his pictures are so amazing.

because it is too tight around your neck.

you will miss them someday.

when I didn't clean my room.

you see your girlfriend smiling at another boy.

she has to be very well prepared.

B. There are many words in the story that are used to talk about feelings. Here is a list of them:

| | |
|---|---|
| love | worried |
| mad | sad |
| excited | scared |
| happy | upset |

166

Separate the words into the two columns and compare your columns with the columns of your partner. Explain your decisions to your partner.

| Good Feelings | Bad Feelings |
|---|---|
|  |  |
|  |  |
|  |  |
|  |  |
|  |  |

C. Finish the sentences below any way you wish. Read your sentences to your partner. Ask your partner questions about his/her sentences.

1. I feel worried when

_____.

2. I used to be happy when

_____.

3. When I was very young, I would be sad when

_____.

4. I used to be excited when

_____.

5. I am proud because

_____.

## ✻ Working with Language

One of the sentences in the story reads "When she came home from work in the evening, the cats *would gather* around her." *Would* and *used to* are two ways of talking about something that happened over and over again in the past. For example, "John *would read* a newspaper every day with his breakfast. He *would always drink* coffee at the same time, but now John has a job that starts very early in the morning, so he reads his newspaper after work."

Think of five things that you would do in the past, but you don't do any longer. Write the five things in the spaces below and then compare your sentences with those of a classmate. Explain to your classmate why you no longer do the things you used to do.

1. I would

   _____.

2. I would

   _____.

3. I would

   _____.

4. I would

   _____.

5. I used to

   _____.

## ✻ Asking Questions

Following are answers to questions. Working with a partner, decide what the questions are. Write your questions in the blank spaces and compare your questions with those of other students.

1. _____?

   At the town's courthouse.

2. _____?

Because he loved Martha.

3. _____?

Because he knew that cats were not good around babies.

4. _____?

Kathleen lost her key.

5. _____?

The cats kept Kathleen warm.

## ❋ Rewriting the Story

Below is the story you just read, only now words are missing from it. Some of the blanks need only one word in them. Others need several words. First, fill in as many of the missing words as you can on your own. Then, working with a classmate, fill in the rest of the blanks to make the story complete. Check this story with the complete story.

## *Martha's* 1. _____ *Cats*

MARTHA KOWALSKI loved cats. She lived alone in a big house filled with cats. Her favorite cats were Attila, Napoleon, and Cuddles. Each cat had his or her own bowl 2. _____ from. The name of each cat was written on his or her bowl, and Martha used to say that her cats 3. _____ how to read because none of them would 4. _____ drink milk from another cat's bowl. Martha's cats were her family. When she came home from work in the evening, the 5. _____ around her. She would pet them, feed them special food, and call them her babies.

Martha worked at the town's 6. _____. She helped lawyers research their cases. One day, she met Lennie O'Conner. Lennie was a new 7. _____. He was tall and handsome, with dark brown eyes and a 8. _____ smile. When he saw Martha, it was love at first sight. He asked her out for dinner, and soon they 9. _____ to all kinds of places together.

One day Lennie and Martha were walking in the park. It was very cold. They both had coats and 10. _____ on, and they were walking very close to each other to stay warm. As they walked, Martha talked about her cats. "Attila has the cutest nose! It always twitches right when she is about to eat, and Napolean never sleeps! Cuddles always needs a hug—"

"You like your cats better than you like me!" Lennie 11. _____. "All you talk about is your cats! Cuddles does this, and Napolean does that!" Lennie was upset.

"I'm sorry, Lennie." Martha didn't know what to do. "I know I talk about my cats a lot, but they are very important to me. My cats are like 12. _____ to me." Lennie listened to Martha talk. He didn't like cats, but he loved Martha, and he knew he would have 13. _____ her cats.

Soon Martha and Lennie 14. _____. They moved into a new house, and Martha brought all her cats. There were so many! Black ones, brown ones, yellow ones, gray ones . . . Lennie felt like they were everywhere! Sometimes he got mad at the cats, but he was very patient and learned 15. _____ with them. Then one day Martha came home with a big smile on her face. "Lennie!" she shouted, very excited. "I'm going 16. _____ a baby!"

Lennie was very happy about the news, but he was also very 17. _____ He knew that cats were not good to have around babies. They slept on top of babies and sometimes smothered them until they 18. _____! Lennie told Martha that she would have to get rid of her cats.

Martha was very sad. She was going to have a baby, but the cats had been her babies for a long time. "Please, Lennie," she said. "Our cats are so smart. I'm sure that they 19. _____ hurt

170

our baby." Lennie thought and thought about it. Finally he agreed that the cats could stay awhile 20. _____.

Kathleen was born in January. She was a beautiful baby girl, with blue eyes and red hair. The cats sniffed at Kathleen, but they didn't think she was much 21. _____. They soon 22. _____ her alone. Kathleen grew bigger, and she played a lot with the cats. Soon Kathleen started going to school. Since her parents worked long hours, Kathleen often 23. _____ home first. She fed the cats, talked to the cats, and treated the cats like part of her family, just like Martha did.

One day Kathleen came home from school and realized that she 24. _____her key to the house. Her parents wouldn't be home from work for another hour, and Kathleen was really 25. _____. It was snowing and very cold. Kathleen didn't know where to go, so she sat down on the porch to wait. Her fingers felt like 26. _____, and her whole body was shaking from the cold. She felt like she 27. _____ right there on the porch. Then Napolean came out of the cat door onto the porch. He sat on Kathleen, his body soft and warm. Then Cuddles came and stretched himself out by Napolean. 28. _____ Attila curled up by Cuddles. Soon all the cats were gathered around Kathleen. Some were sitting on her, some were lying by her, and some were curled up around her feet. They kept Kathleen 29. _____ and happy.

When Lennie came home, Kathleen was 30. _____ on the porch with all the cats around her. Once they found out what happened, Martha laughed. "See, Lennie! Cats don't smother children—they keep them warm inside!" And never again did Lennie tell Martha that she 31. _____ cats.

## ✵ Retelling the Story

Working with a classmate, tell each other the story in your own words. Use the following words and expressions to help you.

| | |
|---|---|
| lived alone | married |
| loved cats | happy news |
| could read | Kathleen |
| when Martha came home | smother |
| her babies | get rid of |
| Lennie | sniffed |
| lawyer | lost her key |
| the park | snowing |
| upset | warm inside |

## ✵ Extending the Story

In small groups, talk about the questions below. Ask one person in your group to take notes, and later tell the class about your talk.

1. Martha loved her cats and they did not hurt baby Kathleen, but many people feel that cats are not nice and cannot be trusted around small children. What do you think? Do you think dogs are better to have around children? Why or why not?

2. At first, Lennie was very upset with the cats, but then he changed his mind. Do you think being in love changes our thoughts about things? Why or why not?

3. Do you think that it is good for children to grow up with animals? Why or why not?

4. Is it good for older people to have pets? Why or why not?

# Looking Back

## ❋ Before You Read

*Talking About the Picture*

Look at the picture. Then, with a partner, answer the questions below. When you have finished talking to your partner, tell the rest of the class what you decided. Listen to the ideas of the other students.

- Where do you think these people are?
- Do you think they're happy?
- How do you think they know each other?
- Many people like riding a bike better than driving a car. Do you agree with them? Why or why not?
- Do people in your country ride bikes? If so, when and why do they bike? If not, why do you think that they don't?

Knowing the words below will help you to understand the story. Listen and repeat as your teacher reads the words. Do you know what these words mean? Ask your teacher or your classmates to help you if you need a meaning explained. Then read the story.

| | |
|---|---|
| honeymoon | to teach someone a lesson |
| romantic | to apologize |
| purchase | fool |
| humid | argument |
| to pedal | scared |
| to avoid | to wave |
| heat | reunited |
| angry | surprised |

## ✳ The Story

# Looking Back

JACK AND SANDY both loved to ride bicycles. They had met in a cycling club and had gone on long bicycle rides all over the world. When they got married they decided that they would go on a bicycling honeymoon in a place where they had never been before. They looked through many travel books and finally decided to go to Taiwan. They heard that in Taiwan people rode on bicycles everywhere—to school, to work, and to stores. 5

Because it was their honeymoon, Jack and Sandy decided to buy a romantic bicycle—a bicycle built for two. They were excited about their new purchase and carried it all the way to Taiwan. 10 When they got to Taiwan, however, they were disappointed. The weather was hot and humid, few people spoke English (and Jack and Sandy didn't speak any Chinese), and worst of all, most people drove cars or motorcycles—hardly anyone rode a bicycle.

Jack and Sandy decided to try and have a good time 15 anyway. Everyone was nice and friendly and they helped answer

174

Jack and Sandy's questions. One day Jack and Sandy decided to
ride their bicycle into the countryside. They left the city and
pedaled down old country roads. This is when they really began to
enjoy their trip. They didn't have to worry as much about
avoiding cars and motorcycles, and the places they went were
beautiful, quiet, and romantic.

Sometimes, however, the heat made Jack and Sandy tired and
angry. During these times, they would start arguing about small
things. One morning they had an argument about a leader of
China. Sandy said that the Chinese leader was just a criminal, but
Jack thought this leader was a great man. They argued past breakfast
time, and were still arguing when they got on their bike. As they
pedaled down the road, the argument got worse and worse. Jack
was really angry, and he started to say things like, "You don't know
anything, Sandy. You don't understand what you are talking about.
Women just don't understand these things."

Sandy listened to Jack and got angrier and angrier, too. She
finally decided to teach Jack a lesson. Without thinking, Sandy
jumped off of the bicycle. She watched Jack continue down the
road. She was sure that Jack would suddenly realize that she wasn't
behind him. She thought of Jack coming back and apologizing.
"Oh, I am so sorry, Sandy," he would say, "I have been such a fool."
But that didn't happen.

Jack was so busy talking and pedaling that he never noticed
that Sandy was no longer behind him. He never looked back, and
he continued to say angry things. In the meantime, Sandy sat down
on the dusty road and began to get scared and sad. She was no
longer angry. She was hot and worried. She couldn't understand
why Jack hadn't come back for her. Maybe he didn't like her
anymore. Maybe a car hit him. Sandy began to cry.

Many people stopped on the road and tried to help Sandy,
but nobody spoke English and Sandy couldn't explain to them what
had happened. Finally a police car stopped. The police officers
couldn't speak English but they had a notepad and a pencil with
them. Sandy drew a picture of the bicycle built for two with only

one person on it. The police officers suddenly understood what had happened. All three started laughing. Poor Sandy!

While Sandy was getting help from the police, Jack was still pedaling and talking. He was surprised that Sandy hadn't said anything back in a very long time. He thought that she wasn't talking because she knew everything he said was right. Suddenly, Jack heard the sound of a police siren behind him. He stopped his bicycle and noticed two things at once: Sandy wasn't on the bike and the policemen in the car were waving at him. Jack was frightened. He didn't understand what was happening. He was scared and worried about Sandy.

The police officers showed Jack the picture that Sandy had drawn. They took Jack to the police station, where he reunited with his wife. Jack and Sandy were both very happy, which really surprised the police officers.

Jack and Sandy enjoyed the rest of their honeymoon like never before. They have been married for ten years now, and whenever they start to argue, one of them says, "Don't forget to look back!" Then they both start laughing, and they soon forget what they were arguing about.

## ❋ Thinking About the Story

### *What Did You Understand?*

A. Answer the following questions in complete sentences. Write your answers in the empty spaces. Then compare your answers with those of a classmate. Your teacher may wish to put these questions on the walls of your classroom and ask you to walk around with a partner answering the questions. Then each of you could take down one question and read it out loud so that the whole class can talk about it.

    1. Why did Sandy and Jack choose Taiwan for their honeymoon?

_____

2. Why were Sandy and Jack disappointed?

_____

3. Why did they like the countryside better than the city?

_____

4. What did they argue about?

_____

5. Why was Sandy angry?

_____

6. Did Sandy have a right to be angry?

_____

7. Why did Sandy decide to jump off the bicycle?

_____

8. What did Sandy think would happen right after she jumped off the bicycle?

_____

9. Why didn't Jack stop?

_____

10. How did Sandy feel when Jack didn't come back?

_____

11. What happened when people tried to help Sandy?

_____

12. How did Sandy explain what had happened to the police officers?

_____

13. Why did the police officers laugh?

_____

14. Why was Jack afraid?

_____

15. Why were the police officers surprised?

_____

B. Correct the sentences below according to the content of the story. Write your corrections in the blanks and compare what you have written with a classmate.

1. Jack and Sandy met in Taiwan.

_____

2. Jack and Sandy decided to go to Thailand for their honeymoon.

_____

3. Jack and Sandy chose Taiwan because the weather there is good.

_____

4. Jack and Sandy saw very few cars in Taiwan.

_____

5. Everyone in Taiwan spoke English.

_____

6. The police officers could not understand why Sandy drew a picture.

_____

## ❋ Working with Words

Jack and Sandy were disappointed when they found out that very few people in Taiwan rode on bicycles. When we put *"dis"* at the beginning of a word, the word often has a negative meaning. Below is a list of words that begin with *"dis"*. Using your dictionary and working with a partner, find the meanings of all the words. Later, use as many of them as you can in sentences.

dislike            _____

disapprove of      _____

displease          _____

discontinue        _____

disadvantage       _____

discharge          _____

dishonest          _____

disaster           _____

disappear          _____

## ❋ Working with Language

Jack and Sandy thought that the worst part of Taiwan was that people had stopped riding bicycles. *Worst* is the strongest way we have of saying that something is bad. When we don't like something, we say that it's *bad*. If we dislike it even more we say that it is *worse*. The thing we dislike the most we say is the *worst* thing. Read the paragraph below and decide which one of the three words (bad, worse, or worst) you want to put in the blanks. Then compare your results with those of a partner.

It rained all day. It was really a boring day. I feel unhappy when the weather is so 1._____, but my neighbor says that last winter the weather was even 2._____. Then it rained for weeks and weeks. My neighbors said it was the 3._____ weather they had ever had in our town. I wasn't here then so I don't know. This is really the 4._____ rain that I have ever seen. My brother, who is a farmer, called me on the telephone. He doesn't think this is the 5. _____ weather he has ever seen. He doesn't think this is 6. _____ weather. He says that the farmers have been waiting for rain for a long time. "This is not the 7. _____ weather I have ever seen," says my brother, the farmer. "This is the best weather for us farmers!"

## ✱ Asking Questions

Following are answers to questions. Working with a partner, decide what the questions are. Write your questions in the blank spaces and compare your questions with those of other students.

1. _____?
   Answer: Because very few people rode bicycles.

2. _____?
   Answer: Because they were so hot and tired.

3. _____?
   Answer: Because they thought this kind of bicycle was romantic.

4. _____?
   Answer: She decided to jump off the bike.

5. _____?
   Answer: Jack continued to argue.

## ✱ Rewriting the Story

Below is the story you just read, only now words are missing from it. Some of the blanks need only one word in them. Others need several words. First, fill in as many of the missing words as you can on your own. Then, working with a classmate, fill in the rest of the blanks to make the story complete. Check this story with the complete story.

# Looking Back

JACK AND SANDY both loved 1. _____ bicycles. They had met in a cycling club and had gone on long bicycle rides all over the world. When they got married they decided that they would go on a bicycling 2. _____ in a place where they had never been before. They looked through many travel books and finally decided to go to 3. _____. They heard that in Taiwan people rode on bicycles everywhere—to school, 4. _____, and to stores.

Because it was their honeymoon, Jack and Sandy decided to buy a 5. _____ bicycle—a bicycle built for two. They were excited about their new purchase and carried it all the way to Taiwan. When they got to Taiwan, however, they were 6. _____. The weather was hot and humid, few people spoke English (and Jack and Sandy didn't speak any 7. _____), and worst of all, most people drove cars or motorcycles—hardly anyone rode a bicycle.

Jack and Sandy decided to try and have a good time anyway. Everyone was nice and 8. _____ and they helped answer Jack and Sandy's questions. One day Jack and Sandy decided to ride their bicycle into the 9. _____. They left the city and 10. _____ down old country roads. This is when they really began to enjoy their 11. _____. They didn't have to worry as much about 12. _____ cars and motorcycles, and the places they went were beautiful, quiet, and romantic.

Sometimes, however, the heat made Jack and Sandy tired and 13. _____. During these times, they would start 14. _____ about small things. One morning they had an 15. _____ about a leader of China. Sandy said that the Chinese leader was just a criminal, but Jack thought this leader was a great man. They argued past breakfast time, and were still arguing when they got on their bike. As they pedaled down the road, the argument got 16. _____. Jack was really angry, and he started to say things like, "You don't know anything, Sandy. You don't understand what you are talking about. Women just don't understand these things."

Sandy 17. _____ Jack and got angrier and angrier, too. She finally decided to teach Jack a 18. _____. Without thinking, Sandy 19. _____ off of the bicycle. She watched Jack continue down the road. She was sure that Jack would suddenly realize that she wasn't behind him. She thought of Jack coming back and 20. _____. "Oh, I am so sorry, Sandy," he would say, "I have been such a 21. _____." But that didn't happen.

Jack was so busy talking and pedaling that he never noticed that Sandy was no longer 22. _____ him. He never 23. _____, and he continued to say angry things. In the meantime, Sandy sat down on the dusty road and began to get scared and sad. She was no longer angry. She was hot and worried. She couldn't 24. _____ why Jack hadn't come back for her. Maybe he didn't like her anymore. Maybe a car hit him. Sandy began 25. _____.

Many people stopped on the road and tried to help Sandy, but nobody spoke 26. _____ and Sandy couldn't 27. _____ to them what had happened. Finally a police car stopped. The police officers couldn't speak English but they had a notepad and a pencil with them. Sandy 28. _____ a picture of the bicycle built for two with only one person on it. The police officers suddenly understood what had happened. All three started 29. _____. Poor Sandy!

While Sandy was getting 30. _____ from the police,

Jack was still pedaling and talking. He was surprised that Sandy hadn't said anything back in a very long time. He thought that she wasn't talking because she knew everything he said was
31. _____. Suddenly, Jack heard the sound of a
32. _____ behind him. He stopped his bicycle and noticed
33. _____ things at once: Sandy wasn't on the bike and the policemen in the car 34. _____ at him. Jack was frightened. He didn't understand what was happening. He was scared and worried about Sandy.

The police officers showed Jack the 35. _____ that Sandy had drawn. They took Jack to the police station, where he 36. _____ with his wife. Jack and Sandy were both very happy, which really surprised the police officers.

Jack and Sandy enjoyed the rest of their honeymoon like never before. They have been married for ten years now, and whenever they start 37. _____, one of them says, "Don't forget to look back!" Then they both start laughing, and they soon forget what they were arguing about.

## ❋ Retelling the Story

Working with a classmate, tell each other the story in your own words. Use the following words and expressions to help you.

> cycling club
> honeymoon
> Taiwan
> school, work, and stores
> disappointed
> nice and friendly
> argue about small things
> great leader
> women just don't understand
> no longer angry

nobody spoke English
police
drew a picture
they were laughing
reunited
don't forget to look back

## ✱ Extending the Story

A. Sandy and Jack are disappointed when they find out that not many people in Taiwan ride bicycles. They probably should have planned their trip better. Below is a list of what people do when they plan for a trip to a different country. In small groups, read the list and talk about the things you would do to prepare for a long trip. Perhaps you would do some things that are not listed here. Tell your group about these things. Ask one person in your group to take notes. Later, ask someone to tell the class what your group has decided are really important things to do before taking a trip to a different country.

Get a passport
Buy suitcases
Get clothes ready
Get a camera
Get the shots you need
Get a guide book
Read about the country you are going to visit
Talk to people from the country you are going to visit
Buy medicines that you need with you
Buy books to read while you travel
Make sure you have a credit card or travelers' checks
Get money from the country you are going to visit
Get a dictionary of the language of that country
Learn how to say some important things in the language that people speak where you are going to visit.

B. Jack and Sandy started arguing about a political leader. People who love each other sometimes argue about things. In small groups talk about the things that people argue about. What are things that make people angry when they talk? Think of good ways to stop an argument. Ask one person in your group to take notes and later tell the rest of the class about your discussion.

C. Jack tells Sandy that women don't understand certain things. This makes Sandy especially angry. In groups, talk about why Sandy is so angry and whether she has the right to get so angry. Then, with your group, write Sandy a letter telling her why you agree or disagree with her. Ask someone in your group to read your letter to the class. (Your teacher may ask you to post your letters on the wall in the classroom, then walk around reading and commenting on the letters that other groups wrote.)

# The Attitude Puzzle

*Answers*

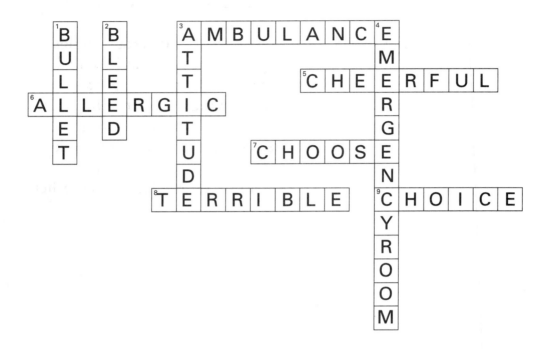

## Across

3. the car that takes you to the hospital
5. puts on a happy face
6. sensitive to something
7. decide what is best
8. the opposite of wonderful
9. the noun of choose

## Down

1. the thing that is fired out of a gun
2. verb from blood
3. the feelings you show
4. place for patients who have not made an appointment

# NOTES

# NOTES

# NOTES

# NOTES

# NOTES

# NOTES

# NOTES

# NOTES

# NOTES

# NOTES

# NOTES

**NOTES**

CANVAS

bFox6706

→ bhelm6706

pW-